THE IDEA OF A NATION

CLASSICS OF IRISH HISTORY

General Editor: Tom Garvin

Other titles in this series:

THE IDEA OF
A NATION

Arthur Clery

edited by
Patrick Maume

University College Dublin Press
Preas Choláiste Ollscoile Bhaile Átha Cliath

This edition first published 2002 by
University College Dublin Press
Introduction © Patrick Maume 2002
The Idea of a Nation first published by
James Duffy & Co. Ltd, Dublin, 1907

ISBN 1 900621 80 0
ISSN 1383–6883

University College Dublin Press
Newman House, 86 St Stephen's Green,
Dublin 2, Ireland
www.ucdpress.ie

Cataloguing in Publication data available from the British Library

Introduction typeset in Ireland in Baskerville
by Elaine Shiels, Bantry, Co. Cork
Printed on acid-free paper in Ireland by Colour Books, Dublin

CONTENTS

INTRODUCTION
Patrick Maume

Arthur Clery
Biographical Note[1]

Arthur Clery was born in Dublin in 1879, only son of Arthur
Clery, barrister, and his wife Catherine (*née* Moylan). His child-
hood was disrupted by a family crisis. His mother suffered a
breakdown and played no further part in his life; his father
repaired the family finances by practising at the Indian Bar.
Clery was brought up in reduced circumstances, assisted by his
cousin Charles Dawson, a former baker and Parnellite politician
turned Dublin Corporation official. (Clery's father retired to
Ireland, learned Irish and became an amateur historian of pre-
conquest Gaelic Ireland as "Art Ua Cleirigh", dying in 1914.
His son greatly respected him and continued to promote his
work. *The Idea of a Nation* is dedicated to him.)

Clery was educated at the Catholic University School in
Leeson Street, run by the Marist Fathers (his confirmation
name and favourite pen-name derived from the French Marist
martyr Pierre Chanel), Clongowes (1894–6) and the Jesuit-run
University College, precursor of University College Dublin
(1896–1900). Throughout his career Clery's social life revolved
around his cohort of Clongownians and University College
graduates (which included Tom Kettle and the future Chief
Justice Hugh Kennedy). From them was recruited the twelve-
member Cui Bono, a dining-club whose leading figures were
Kettle and Clery. Clery was active in Clongowes and University

College Dublin alumni groups, and a lifelong participant in Catholic social work in inner-city Dublin through the Society of St Vincent de Paul. In the 1920s he was a founder member of An Rioghacht, a group which promoted Catholic social doctrine and became the Catholic Social Services Conference.

Clery was prominent in University College's debating society, the Literary and Historical Society, where he delivered (11 February 1899) a paper declaring that Ireland needed a national drama and that all true drama was religious drama. A student two years his junior, James Joyce, replied with a paper on "Drama and Life" declaring Ibsen the first true dramatist because he emphasised the individual conscience. College authorities initially banned Joyce's paper as heterodox (the decision was conveyed by the auditor—Clery), but this was reversed after Joyce appealed to the college president. Clery's occasional later references to Joyce combine insistence that the disreputable medical students of *Portrait of the Artist*, though accurately portrayed, represent only a small and unrepresentative section of his generally pious and moral contemporaries at University College[2] with embarrassment that one of the few high-profile Clongowes literary figures should have been so morally dubious.[3] Although Joyce wrote to Clery thanking him for a favourable review of his early book of verse, *Chamber Music* (1907), Clery was lampooned in the unpublished *Stephen Hero* as "Whelan, the college orator".[4]

At the beginning of his college career Clery fancied himself as a dandy and paraded his affection for the eighteenth-century Anglo-Irish literary tradition and the writings of Thackeray.[5] (He always revered Swift as a fellow-journalist.) In 1897 he joined the Gaelic League, studying the standard textbooks written by Fr. Eugene O'Growney (pp. 40–3) and attending Pearse's modh-reidh Irish-language classes (p. 6) which employed "direct method" language learning, based on con-versation. This led to a thoroughgoing conversion to "Irish Ireland" under the influence of D. P. Moran.

After graduation Clery became a barrister; his courtroom manner was unimpressive and he supplemented his earnings by journalism. From 1902 he was a regular contributor to Moran's weekly *Leader* under the pen name "Chanel"; *The Idea of a Nation* is a selection of these pieces. Clery also wrote for the *New Ireland Review* as "Arthur Synan"; his only novel, *The Return of the King*, appeared under that name in 1907. A second collection, *Dublin Essays*, appeared in 1920.

In 1912 Clery became part-time Professor of the Law of Property at University College Dublin; his pupils included John A. Costello. He joined the Irish Volunteers in 1914 and supported Eoin MacNeill when the movement split over Redmond's support for the Allied war effort. After the Easter Rising Clery was defence counsel at MacNeill's court martial. He was one of the few barristers to work with the Sinn Féin courts system (risking disbarment). He was entrusted with the funds of the underground Land Bank, and in 1920 Austin Stack appointed him to the underground Supreme Court.

Clery opposed the Treaty, saying the Free State was not genuinely independent and would be reabsorbed through corruption and West Britonism. At the inception of the Civil War, Clery and another Republican judge attempted to force the release of Republicans captured in the battle for Dublin; the court was dissolved by the Free State government. Clery went to Rome with Dr. Con Murphy to put the Republican case to the Vatican. Their complaints led to the despatch of a Papal Nuncio, Mgr. Luzio; Clery arranged a clandestine meeting with de Valera.[6]

Clery refused a Free State judicial pension, although his legal income was severely restricted by the rule that former judges do not appear before courts inferior to that on which they served. He refused to submit income tax returns to a state which he thought illegitimate; the state taxed him as if he had actually received the pension for which he was eligible.

As one of the few University College Dublin staff members to oppose the Treaty, Clery chaired the University's Republican Club (which included Fianna Fáilers and Sinn Féiners). In June 1927 he was elected to a National University of Ireland Dáil seat as an Independent Republican (defeating MacNeill).

Clery refused to take the Oath of Allegiance when it became compulsory for Dáil membership, and did not contest the September 1927 election. Thereafter he acted as occasional legal adviser to both Fianna Fáil (he provided de Valera with a legal opinion that the Free State was not bound to pay the Land Annuities to Britain) and Sinn Féin (he advised Mary MacSwiney on drafting a Republican constitution).

Despite the respect of surviving friends (even political opponents) and the admiration of his students, Clery's last years were austere and melancholy. He died in November 1932 from pneumonia contracted at a political meeting. Much of his leisure time was devoted to exercise in an attempt to cope with his weight problem; most of his estate went to provide sports facilities for UCD students. He was commemorated by a plaque in the rowing club's boathouse at Islandbridge, and the tennis courts were named after him.[7]

The Idea of a Nation

Clery's life was shaped by two political projects dating back to the first half of the nineteenth century. The first was the endeavour of the Catholic senior clergy to create a class of Catholic professionals responsive to clerical guidance, who would service the Catholic population and influence the Irish administration in accordance with the Church's interests. This reflected fear that the British state (whose sense of identity was strongly bound up with Protestantism) and the Irish Protestant minority (with its disproportionate wealth and political influence) might undermine Irish Catholicism by underwriting service provision by evangelising Protestant groups or producing a Continental-style anti-clerical intelligentsia through secular education.

The development of a Catholic professional elite was furthered by the Intermediate Education (Ireland) Act of 1878, which financed denominational secondary schools by awarding state scholarships to pupils on the basis of state examinations. Annual examination results became a focus for competition between rival schools and denominations. Examination results were deployed in the long running debate about the Catholic hierarchy's supreme educational objective—control of the whole process of professional formation through a state-funded Catholic university on an equal footing with Trinity College, Dublin. Much of Clery's early journalism discusses the "University Question" and the job prospects of University College graduates as compared to their Trinity contemporaries. He was particularly angry that well-off Catholics, like Sir Christopher Nixon, Master of the Catholic University School of Medicine, whose supple consciences allowed them to send their own children to Trinity received positions of honour in church-sponsored campaigns for a Catholic University while poorer Catholics were expected to refrain from competing for well-funded Trinity scholarships. (Cf. "Going to Trinity" pp. 29–33.)[8]

The Intermediate scheme had the advantages and demerits of meritocracy. It provided a relatively straightforward and transparent test of ability, and when combined with the increased opening of Civil Service positions to competitive examinations did much to correct under-representation of Catholics and Presbyterians in professional and administrative positions. Critics ranging from Pearse to the ex-Clongownian agnostic Francis Hackett complained that it focused on a narrow curriculum which privileged the professions and concentrated on passing exams at the expense of the pupil's broader development, with the relationship between boy, school, and parents often distorted by an emphasis on prize-winning.[9]

The Catholic professional project co-existed uneasily with the nationalist political project which, when Clery attended Clongowes, had found its most recent expression in the movement led by Parnell. Nationalist opposition to taking official positions until Home Rule was granted sat uneasily with hopes for Catholic permeation of the system; nationalist demands for confrontation with the administration created tension with clerical hopes for winning concessions from government. With more Catholic professionals being trained than Ireland could accommodate, Britain and its empire offered professional opportunity (and the prospect of strengthening the Church abroad). Catholicism, as a hierarchical religion, could be seen as inculcating deference. Many Catholic land-owners and professionals were Unionists (from conservatism, snobbery, self-interest, and genuine concern at the limitations of the nationalist leadership) as were some of the secular and religious priests who serviced them. A significant minority of pupils and teachers at Clongowes in Clery's day were Unionists. The expectation among University College Dublin students in 1911–12 that their undergraduate debates were the training-ground for a College Green Parliament[10] should not necessarily be attributed to Clery's generation. The arguments against imperialism and in favour of nationalism put forward in *The Idea of a Nation* were written by someone for whom Unionism or emigration had been serious career options, whose formative years witnessed the high point of Imperial confidence and the squalid political factionalism after the fall of Parnell.

Nonetheless Clery accepted the nationalist view that the professional difficulties of young Irish graduates and the eco-nomic stagnation of Edwardian Dublin both derived from the Union, and those who accepted the status quo were parasites who throve at their country's expense. He chose professional self-sacrifice with a zeal reinforced by the religious asceticism of his teachers. Despite his fervent Catholicism Clery always regarded himself as a Parnellite; in his subsequent opposition to the Treaty he referred back to the Parnellite belief that the anti-Parnellites forfeited the opportunity of Home Rule in the 1890s through weakness and jobbery. He commented bitingly on Catholic snobs, lay and clerical, who deferred to aristocrats who despised them and sneered at the "agitators" who won them access to the positions which they enjoyed. One of Clery's few luxuries was a fondness for European travel; his ideas on partition were influenced by observing ethnic divisions in the Tyrol during a ski-ing trip with Kettle. His belief in "looking beyond England" to Catholic Europe and German Idealism (shared with Kettle and their contemporary, the Heidelbergtrained philosopher John Marcus O'Sullivan) reflected a growing self-confidence among younger Catholic intellectuals.

Kettle and his contemporaries in the Young Ireland Branch of the United Irish League tried to infuse the Irish Party with new ideas. Clery took a more detached attitude. (He noted the provincial patronage rings of local Party bosses as an obstacle faced by graduates seeking employment.) Instead, he turned to the cultural nationalism advanced by D. P. Moran, who added to Douglas Hyde's view of the Gaelic heritage as fundamental to Irish self-respect and well-being an insistence that to be Gaelic was to be Catholic and "the Gael must be the element that absorbs". Moran's posthumous reputation is dominated by his sectarianism and his considerable addition to the streams of verbal abuse which polluted Irish political discourse; but he was also a shrewd publicist and social observer. His admirers, who included Clery, venerated him as a teller of awkward truths. Clery never succeeded in learning Irish, but treasured his regular visits to the Gaeltacht and contact with its people, and praised the zeal for self-improvement shown by the plebeian enthusiasts who attended the classes of the early Gaelic League.

For thirty years Clery commented on Irish life in the *Leader*, only a fraction of his pieces were published in book form. They make engaging, if uneven, reading. Clery retained some characteristics of the student debater: flippancy and desire to impress, reaching for big ideas without fully understanding them, fondness for the grand peroration (p. 36). His denunciations of snobbery were excessively self-conscious; C. S. Andrews, who knew the older Clery in the 1920s, noted that he retained distinct traces of snobbery. At the same time, Clery generalised from his experience of subordination as an Irish Catholic to attack other forms of oppression, even when much Catholic opinion favoured them. He was an outspoken supporter of women's suffrage (he believed women were more religious and moral than men and would improve public life). He denounced corporal punishment in schools (his old teacher and fellow University College Dublin professor, Fr. Timothy

Corcoran SJ, believed that those who questioned corporal punishment denied Original Sin), though his suggestion that it might be abolished by lowering the voting age to seven (the Catholic age of reason) overshadowed his other arguments. Clery compared the oppressive reactionary politics espoused by many French Catholics to the aristocratic snobbery of Trinity College, and suggested that the French Church might learn by the Irish example of combining Catholicism with democracy. Clery even criticised Belloc and Chesterton (whom he revered) for their anti-semitism, pointing out affinities between hostile stereotypes of Jews and of Irish Catholics. (This did not prevent him making anti-semitic remarks about Sir Matthew Nathan in 1914.)[11]

The ungainly, unmarriageable misfit could be a shrewd social observer. *The Idea of a Nation* provides glimpses of the atmosphere of the early Irish Revival: concerts in draughty halls listening to the traditional singing of Seamus Clandillon (subsequently first Director of the Irish radio station 2RN); the contrast between big words and token gestures at Gaelic League rallies (parodied, along with Unionism, in "The Revival of English"); contemptuous glances at "West British clerks" flirting in tea-shops; the inverted snobbery of determinedly "unrespectable" Gaelic Leaguers; hopes that the Abbey might produce the religious folk-drama of which the student Clery had dreamed giving way to disquiet at Yeats's assertions during the controversies surrounding *Shadow of the Glen*[12] and sarcastic comments on the gap between Yeats's ambitions for his short poetic dramas and their position as curtain-raisers to popular kitchen comedies.

Several early pieces discussing why many Protestants underwent brief youthful flirtations with nationalism before reverting to Unionism contain subtle explorations of the invisible social barriers within Dublin middle-class society, and the particular combination of pride in Ireland and attachment to the Union found in many Edwardian Protestants. Clery reminded readers who wondered at Protestant support for the Union that Grattan's Parliament brought many economic benefits; yet what Irish Catholic would support Home Rule if it meant subjugation to a Protestant Parliament? Was it not natural that Protestants should fear rule by a Catholic majority which might not persecute them, but whose outlook and assumptions were in many ways directly opposed to their own? (In Clery's later writings this openness gives way to bitter mumblings about Masonic plots.)

In this spirit Clery developed the most distinctive position expressed in these essays: the view that Ulster Unionists were a separate nation and districts where they formed a majority should be partitioned from a Home Rule Ireland and remain attached to Great Britain. Other nationalist observers saw the rebellion of the Orange rabble-rousers, T. H. Sloan and Arthur Trew, against the aristocratic official Unionism of Edward Saunderson and the support of some southern land-lords (notably Lord Dunraven) for devolution as signs that Unionism was disintegrating; Clery realised they marked the emergence of a populist Ulster Unionism increasingly detached from its southern counterpart. Clery glossed over some awkward points (notably the position of Belfast Catholics), but addressed issues which most other nationalists evaded until they were forced on them. His partitionism arose from recognition that the same arguments nationalists employed to defend their own political aspirations obliged them to treat the loyalties of Ulster Unionists seriously.[13] This willingness to address awkward questions and address an alien viewpoint entitles Clery to recognition as a notable commentator on the Ireland of his day.

Most of these essays first appeared in the *Leader* between 1902 and 1907. This edition adds Clery's review of *Chamber Music*, his original partitionist statement in the *New Ireland Review* (a precursor of *Studies* which allowed him more space than the *Leader*) and an article on his educational experiences repro-duced by the *Mayo News* in 1919, apparently from an issue of the *Leader* missing from the National Library of Ireland.

Two more articles show Clery's views on partition at a later stage, when he had become embittered by the political upheavals after 1912. An attack on the 1917–18 Irish Convention as undemocratic highlights the link between Clery's partitionism and his belief that his professional advancement had been hindered by his political and religious views, while an article written in response to the Irish Parliamentary Party's defeat of Sinn Féin in 1918 is the most strident expression of his lifelong dislike of Ulster Catholics. A review of Daniel Corkery's *Synge and Anglo-Irish Literature* gives the ageing and embittered Clery's final thoughts on the early years of the Abbey Theatre, and serves as a reminder that Corkery's book, though widely and understandably seen as an attack on Synge, was actually intended as a defence of him against harsher nationalist critics.

1   For Clery and his milieu see C. P. Curran, *Under the Receding Wave* (Dublin, 1970), pp. 125–37; Patrick Maume, "Nationalism and partition: the political thought of Arthur Clery", *Irish Historical Studies*, November 1998; Patrick Maume, *The Long Gestation: Nationalist Political Life 1891–1918* (Dublin, 1999); Senia Paseta *Before the Revolution: Nationalism, Social Change, and Ireland's Catholic Elite, 1879–1922* (Cork, 1999). I am grateful to Eugene McNulty, University of Kent at Canterbury, for inviting me to give a paper on Clery (which formed the basis for this introduction) to his seminar in April 2001.

2   Arthur Clery, *Dublin Essays* (Dublin, 1920), p. 56n.

3   [William Menton, compiler], *The Clongowes Union Centenary Chronicle* (Clongowes, 1997), pp. 226, 227, 229. Clery suggested Joyce was more a Belvederian than a Clongownian.

4   For the Joyce–Clery relationship see Richard Ellmann, *James Joyce* (rev. ed. Oxford, 1982), pp. 70, 73, 90, 261; Stanislaus Joyce, *My Brother's Keeper: James Joyce's Early Years* (New York, 1958), pp. 113, 144; Curran, *Under the Receding Wave*, pp. 125–6. Clery reprinted his paper on the theatre in *Dublin Essays* (Dublin, 1920), pp. 114–21. Its call for a religious folk-art is echoed in the present volume's call for a national religious art ("Art and Nationality", pp. 19–23), which also reflects a campaign in the *Leader* by Edward Martyn and the Celtic Revivalist art critic Robert Elliott. Clery's hopes for a religious folk-theatre may have influenced his refusal to sign the 1899 student petition denouncing Yeats's *Countess Cathleen*.

5   A relic of this enthusiasm is the 1899 student paper "Irish Genius in English Prose", reprinted with a disclaimer in *Dublin Essays*, pp. 83–92.

6   Patrick Murray, *Oracles of God: The Roman Catholic Church and Irish Politics, 1922–37* (Dublin, 2000), pp. 180–5.

7 Donal McCartney, *UCD: A National Idea* (Dublin, 1999), p. 117. Clery devoted some effort to arguing that tennis was not covered by the ban on foreign games.

8 For Nixon see F. O. C. Meenan, *Cecilia Street: The Catholic University School of Medicine 1855–1931* (Dublin, 1987), especially p. 77.

9 P. H. Pearse, *The Murder Machine* (first pub. 1916) in Seamas Ó Buachalla (ed.), *A Significant Irish Educationalist: The Educational Writings of P.H. Pearse* (Cork, 1980). Francis Hackett *The Green Lion* (London, 1936), a semi-autobiographical novel, sardonically contrasts the college's traditional Jesuit educational terminology and its preoccupation with the Intermediate examinations.

10 James Meenan, *George O'Brien: A Biographical Memoir* (Dublin, 1980), pp. 33–4.

11 Ben Novick, *Conceiving Revolution: Irish Nationalist Propaganda during the First World War* (Dublin, 2001), pp. 134–5.

12 "The Philosophy of an Irish Theatre" appeared in the *Leader* on 31 October 1903; the reference to the *Playboy* is a later addition. Clery responds to Yeats's manifesto in *Samhain* (R. F. Foster, *W.B. Yeats: A Life – I: The Apprentice Mage* (London, 1997), pp. 298–300. Between 1902 and 1907, Clery was the *Leader*'s chief drama critic; he admired Lady Gregory's *Kincora* (1905) as the theatre's "first undoubted masterpiece" while denouncing Synge as pagan and nihilistic.

13 The most prominent reply to Clery, Eoin MacNeill, *Shall Ireland Be Divided?* (Dublin, 1916) has shrewd observations on Ulster society and the difficulty of drawing a workable border, but resorts to facile dismissal of popular Unionism as irrational and ephemeral.

NOTE ON THE TEXT

The text of *The Idea of a Nation* has been printed as a facsimile of the first edition of the book, published by James Duffy and Co. Ltd, Dublin, 1907. The other writings by Arthur Clery, originally published in the *Leader* and elsewhere, have been re-set.

THE
IDEA OF A NATION.

BY

C H A N E L.

Dublin:

JAMES DUFFY AND CO., Limited,

15 Wellington Quay.

———

1907.

Dedication.

———◆———

ᴅᴜɪᴛ-ꜱᴇ, ᴀ ᴀᴛ́ᴀɪʀ,

ᴅᴏ

ꜰóᵹʟᴜɪᴍ ᴀɴ ᵹᴀᴇᴅ́ɪʟᴢᴇ

ɪᴀ⅂ᴦ ᴍʙᴇɪᴛ́

ᴛʀ́ɪ ꜰɪᴄ́ᴇᴀᴅ ʙʟɪᴀᴅ́ᴀɪɴ

ᴅ'ᴀᴏɪꜱ.

PREFACE.

"Do cum ᵹlóiʃe Dé aᵹuʃ onóʃa na h-Éiʃeann."

Two of these essays are now put forth for the first time, the others have appeared at intervals during the past five years in the columns of *The Leader*, and are now republished with some slight alterations. In the profound intellectual movement for which *The Leader* has been responsible in this country, my own part has been a trifling one; everyone recognises that it is to the originality and striking personal character of its editor, Mr. D. P. Moran, that, beyond all else, its influence has been due. It is, however, no small pleasure to have contributed to a paper that has so deeply affected Irish thought and activity in our own time—more deeply, indeed, than most men are now ready to acknowledge. A number of the Articles which I contributed to it dealt directly or indirectly with the subject of Irish Nationality. These I have now brought together, and added two others, so as to afford a connected treatment of that important subject. In doing so I seek to deal primarily with the idea of nationhood as touching our own country, but also, though in a less degree, with that idea as affecting the actions of all civilised human beings at the present day. Some thinkers may disapprove of national feeling or seek to repress it ; but it is only in Ireland that men scoff at it or affect to ignore it. My treatment of this difficult problem may not always be adequate ; I can only urge as excuse that I have directed my efforts to make it as far as possible popular.

CHANEL.

THE IDEA OF A NATION.

———◆———

I.—On Tram-Car's Top.

T was on a tram-car. The Boer war was still in progress. They were passing the Gaelic League offices. The traveller returned from England, was fain to know what d—— nonsense was written up there. The satisfaction of his curiosity by his patient Irish acquaintance only served to raise his ire. A discussion on the Irish language naturally followed. The people's time was being wasted. French was more useful. It was a cruel wrong to deprive the children of a glorious commercial future. What good was it to anyone? Of course he spoke as the friend of Ireland; he had been in England, and had learned sense (thank God!). Discussion between people who have no idea in common seldom remains amicable; so the quiet man said little, but let the conversation work round from "the Irish language" (at the Pillar) to "language" (at O'Connell-bridge), and finally (as they passed through College-green) to Nationality. At last the man from England sought to settle matters by an aphorism.

A. "Nationality's all b—— humbug."

B. "I suppose then you'd think it very foolish for an Englishman to volunteer and get killed in the war."

A. "Oh! fighting for your country's different."

B. "What do you mean by 'your country' then?"

A. "What's the '——' use of asking silly questions. The place where you're born of course."

B. "Your father was born in India, wasn't he? I suppose he sided with his Hindu fellow-countrymen in the mutiny."

A. "Not d—— likely. Of course your country's the same, even out there."

B. "Then it isn't the place you're born in that matters."

A. "Well, of course, it's as if you were born in England, you know."

B. "England and India being the same place?"

A. "Oh! well, it's the English Empire out there just the same. I suppose I was wrong in talking about 'place.' The niggers were disloyal, and, of course, it was his duty to support the government."

B. "So your country really means your government."

A. "More or less."

B. "And it's for your government, and not for the land you're born in, you should fight. We're agreed on that."

A. "I suppose so."

B. "And the Boers, of course, should fight for the English Government?"

A. "Why not?"

B. "And the Irish?"

A. "Of course they would. I should anyway, and I am as good an Irishman as any man."

B. "So if England were conquered by France, you'd fight for the French, and join in putting down English rebellions."

A. "I'd see them in —— first, Of course, I'd fight for my own country."

B. "But England would not be your country."

A. "What nonsense! Why shouldn't it be, even then?"

B. "Why we agreed that your country meant your government."

A. " Did we ?   Perhaps we did.   But you wouldn't have been born a ' Froggy,' would you, now ? "

B. " So it 's the government you 're born under that matters."

A. " That 's more like it."

B. " Then it would be your sons' duty to help the French in keeping you and other Englishmen down."

A. " Talk sense. They'd never be so unpatriotic ? "

B. " Patriotic !   But that means loving your country, doesn't it ? "

A. " I suppose it does."

B. " Then as lovers of their country—which means, as you say, the government they were born under— they ought to fight for the French."

A. " You 're a "——" awful quibbler. You know that 's rubbish, yourself."

B. " I do ; but doesn't it follow from your defini- tion of country ? "

A. " D—— definitions."

B. " Might it not be better to find out where we 're wrong ? "

A. " You see it 's this way—the English Johnnies could never be the same as the frog-eating French. Fancy gobbling snails !   Ha, ha !   There 'd always be a big difference."

B. " Of what ?   Clothes, stature, diet, perhaps ? "

A. " Oh, more than that ; a whole lot of things. They speak a different lingo, for one."

B. " But teach the English French ; then there 'd be no difference."

A. "Um! perhaps after a long time there wouldn't; but it would take a —— long time to make the mixture."

B. " So, then, there 's a difference very hard to destroy ? "

A. " There is, isn't there."

B. " Partly language, partly other things."

A. " So I said."

B. " And that 's what makes ' your country'?"

A. " It 's about that."

B. " When you say you 'd fight for your country, then, you really mean you 'd fight for certain people having these peculiarities ?"

A. " I suppose so."

B. " You 'd do other things as well as fight, for your country ?"

A. " Of course."

B. " Then these peculiarities are important ?"

A. " They are, aren't they ?"

B. " But mightn't they be called Nationality ?"

A. " Well, I suppose they might. I was not think-ing of that—forgot we were talking about it."

B. " So Nationality 's not humbug ?"

A. " I suppose not."

B. " Nor b—— humbug ?"

A. " No."

B. " beannaċt leac."

[It was Merrion Square.]

II.—Nationhood and Politics.

THE opposition between nationality and national-ism has been a common topic of discussion in recent years. A grave hostility between the old and the new species of nationalist has often been arrived at upon theoretical grounds, and has now and then shown itself in practice. There is indeed no small difference between the meaning of "nation," "national," "anti-Irish," "West-British," and similar terms, as they are used by the younger men of our own day, and the signification of the same words on the lips of our fathers twenty years ago; and the reason of this difference is to be found in the uprise of the Irish movement. The new ideas were thought out in the musty precincts of the early Gaelic League; and they penetrated into men's reluctant consciences in large part through the moral surgery of *The Leader* newspaper. But the new-point of view has now become so much an accepted fact, that it is not always easy to realise how startling was the novelty, a few years ago, of doctrines, which the younger generation of Irishmen have come to look upon as first principles.

It is not that we are better or braver men than our fathers. It was our very weakness that threw us back upon reflection and lead us to see things more clearly than they did, to see how foolish was the policy inaugurated by O'Connell, of allowing the Irish people to abandon every intellectual trust, if only they kept the powder dry. But once we did reflect, the truth was clear, that nationality was not a matter of mere political or other polemics, but that if we would fight on behalf of our nation, we must see that the nation, the thing itself that was the cause of our efforts, did not perish in our rear, while we were out battling for it in the field.

For nationhood is not a mere question of colour on the map, still less a question of coloured squares on the result map of a general election. A nation is an entity, that has its essence in the mind, but is founded on language, habits, customs, tradition, and common history. It is the largest extension of individual love and hope, and like a faith it may crumble away before slow assault, and at last be dissolved in chill, formless nothingness. And this was what was happening in Ireland. We fought England as fiercely as ever, but all the time we were sinking into landless men, with nothing to rally round save an historic flag. Our ardour was not lessened, but everything that was distinctively Irish was passing from us, and instead of Irish patriots. as we thought ourselves, we were becoming merely a discontented body of Britons. We might draw a comparison from the kindred ideal of religion. In the Irish nation the state of affairs had become not unlike that of a body of men combating fiercely on behalf of their creed while they were themselves day by day losing the faith.

These doctrines are not very new to-day, but when the *Philosophy of Irish Ireland* was written and in the years before it, your ordinary man found them very hard to accept, nor has the older generation in our own time even yet thoroughly assimilated them, and it is this latter fact and not any real innate antagonism that sometimes brings politician and Gaelic Leaguer into conflict. The politician very often cannot understand or realise why others are dissatisfied with his conduct. Is he not doing his part and why should he be asked to do more? When he spends the day fighting for the faith, it is surely churlish to inquire about his personal character or his evening prayers. Considerations of bad example don't appeal to him, and he has an angry sense, that his critics are fighting the battle of the other side. For few things are more irritating than to be told that you have not done enough. We can hardly be astonished, then, if the politician receives any suggestion that his abundant spare hours at Westminster might be filled up by a móὐ-ῃéῐὐ class, and hallowed by a Father Cullen badge, with a ferocious growl of middle-aged self-righteousness.

On the other hand it is a galling doctrine to the Nationalist politician and a very suspicious one to the malevolent onlooker, that one may be "national" without being a nationalist. Of course this is the strict theoretic truth; one may love the Irish people and desire that they remain the Irish people in the fullest sense of the word, preserving their national integrity in thought, literature, language and all else, and yet at the same time believe in any political doctrines whatsoever. If only a man desire the welfare and spiritual integrity —very few Unionists do in fact desire the latter— of his nation, he is national ; though the means he may approve for promoting that welfare and and integrity may vary infinitely, from presenting petitions to the Lord Lieutenant to arranging for dynamite explosions.

But though there may be nothing irrational in a man of national sentiments being a Unionist or worse, the two points of view not being contradictory, it may none the less, be, and in the opinion of most men is, unnatural and unwise that he should be such. And in practice men who have accepted the national view in intellectual matters, usually adopt some form of nationalist politics. There is no reason why an Englishman should not be at the same time a Nonconformist and a Unionist. The two bodies of opinion are not contradictory. But to-day every Nonconformist chapel in England is in an indirect way a recruiting ground for political Liberalism. And the relation of the Gaelic League towards Nationalist Politics is precisely the same. It is not a political organisation ; men of all shades of nationalist opinion belong to it, together with a certain number of Unionists. But very few men who love Ireland and the intellectual integrity of its people can find life tolerable in the Unionist camp for very long. He was not a cruel or unloving father, who in the old story imprisoned his daughter in a brazen tower. And the Unionist that yet loves Ireland is his like. But common sense will prevent there being ever many such.

III.—The Theory of Nationhood.

SCENE : *The Rotunda* (Shilling-place).

(Three students, one a philosopher, discovered. Excursions and alarms without.)

Ꮽꞃc.—Are they ever going to begin ?

Seaᵹán.—Be patient. Why it's only 8 o'clock, the hour it was advertised for. It ought to start in another twenty minutes or so.

Ꮽꞃc.—That's always the way with Gaelic concerts. The habits of our nation, I suppose.

Sea.—(After a pause) " Habit of our nation;" now, what does that really mean ?

Ꮽꞃc.—Oh, you're at philosophy again. Why, isn't it plain enough ?

Sea.—Well, I hope you know what you understand by habit. But what do you mean by "nation"?

Ꮽꞃc.—Oh, I read that dialogue the other day; we 're not on a tram-car now.

Sea.—I am not trying to catch you ; I am really seriously in doubt as to what nation means.

Seumuꞃ.—I 'd like to be a little clearer on it myself.

Ꮽꞃc.—Yet you 've both come to this ꞃꞬoꞃuɩꝺeaċc.

Sea.—Oh, I recognise the existence of nationhood and certainly of an Irish nation in practice, but when I try to work it out in theory, it 's not easy to discover what exactly is this thing " nation" we all talk about so much.

Ꮽꞃc.—See the dangers of philosophical study.

Sea.—You can't turn it off by a joke.

Seu.—Suppose we occupy this most useful interval by trying to find out what it means. Now, I am inclined to think that it is language that makes the nation.

Seᴀ.—Do you mean that all people speaking different languages belong to different nations?

Seu.—I think so.

Seᴀ.—Would you say, then, that my grandmother, who spoke Irish, belonged to a different nation from myself, as I speak English?

Seu.—I would have to.

Seᴀ.—Then, what becomes of your Irish nation?

Seu.—That's certainly a difficulty. Suppose we only say, then, that all who speak the same language belong to the same nation.

Seᴀ.—That's absurd. Do you consider that your fellow-citizens of the United States (you had the misfortune to be born there)—

Seu.—That does not count.

Seᴀ.—are the same nation as the English?

Seu.—I'm very much afraid they are.

Seᴀ—I don't think so at all. Though they are a special case, they are, or at any rate they're becoming, a nation.

Seu.—Let us try and get some other example, then, that we can agree on.

Seᴀ.—You've rushed to your own destruction. Would you say that the Irish-speaking Galway man belongs to the same nation as the Scotch Highlander, and to a different nation from the English-speaking Roscommon man?

Aᴘᴛ.—Surely you wouldn't consider the French, the French Canadians, the Belgians and the Western Swiss as all belonging to the same nation. If you used the word "nation" in this way you'd really be using it in quite a different sense.

Seᴀ.—Ridiculous! my dear boy!

Seu.—You're both on me now. I am afraid I'd never be able to overcome two such orators, so, perhaps, you'd each tell me what you think it means?

Seᴀ.—Well, perhaps, you'll disagree; but it seems to me that the word "nation" covers a lot of things. I don't think it has any one fixed meaning.

Aɼc.—How do you mean? Do you hold there is no such thing?

Seá.—Oh, no. There's an Irish nation, a French nation, a Polish nation; but the word in each case means quite a different thing. In one case language; in another political unity, and so on.

Seu.—But you destroy the whole theory. If there is no common thing, why delude ourselves by using a common name?

Aɼc.—Our friend does not see he has really denied the doctrine altogether.

Seá.—Not at all. I am quite as enthusiastic on behalf of our " language, religion, sentiment," nation as the French on behalf of their political nation. Else, why should I be sitting in the draught of that door?

Seu.—We acknowledge your heroic spirit, but we think you've abandoned the only true justification for it. Surely in all these cases, though the features of each are different, there is a common element, the thing called nationhood, in all.

Seá.—I don't admit there is anything common— that is, except the word.

Seu.—Well, I am sure you will permit us to differ from you, though we are not all philosophers.

Aɼc.—Hello! there's Clandillon coming out.

Seu.—We must adjourn our symposium.

Seá.—Suiö ɼíoɼ. Suiö ɼíoɼ.

* * * * * * *

Seu. 7 Aɼc.—Aɼíɼ, aɼíɼ.

Seu.—There's no good, he won't give a third.

Aɼc.—Confound you philosophers, why didn't you join us and show some enthusiasm.

Seá.—I suppose you'll tell me I'm anti-national.

Apc.—You are.

Sea.—Now, do you mean anti-Irish-national or anti-French-national?

Apc.—There are limits to human endurance.

Seu.—Peace, my brothers. He only wants us to go on with the argument.

Sea.—If you're not going out during the interval I suppose we may as well.

Seu.—I was thinking over it while Clandillon was singing. It seemed to me that after all traditional singing was quite as much an essential of nationality as anything else.

Sea.—New definition of nationality.

Apc.—Surely you wouldn't call a thing which is so small compared with, say, political freedom, language, or that sort of thing, an essential?

Seu.—Well, in a way I'd call everything essential.

Apc.—How so?

Seu.—I was just thinking that nationality is a sum total, the aggregate of qualities, experiences, and characteristics.

Sea.—What's a nation then?

Seu.—A nation, I would say, is a body that, as the result of continued existence, has collected and retains a sufficient sum total of such qualities and characteristics, say for instance, common language, history, manners, traditions, music, and so on. You might even consider rudeness as a part of English nationhood.

Apc.—Do you believe any of them essential?

Seu.—No; I think the presence of a certain number of them makes up the nation.

Apc.—Perhaps you are right. But by your method we can never fix on anything; we can never know what a nation exactly is. We can never have a test.

Sea.—That's just it. Would you consider clothing or cooking elements of nationality?

Seu.—Of course, these are some difficulties, but can you fellows suggest a better description?

Ꭺꞃꞇ.—I think I can. We have only to push your argument further.

Seu.—I don't follow.

Ꭺꞃꞇ.—What you call nationality is really only what produces it. It's not the talking Irish or the traditional singing that makes up nationality, but nationality is the common feeling, the continued moral and intellectual sympathy that can only arise in a people by having a common language, common traditions, and such like. It comes as the result of them.

Seꭺ.—You agree, then, that nationality is a different thing in every case?

Ꭺꞃꞇ.—Not at all. It arises from different causes; but the bond of sympathy, the community of sentiment in which it consists, is always essentially the same.

Seu.—What example would you give?

Ꭺꞃꞇ.—Take Switzerland. Like your fatherland, the United States, it is composed of different racial stocks—French, German, and Italian. Common history, common interest, common trials have welded it into that band of men having common sympathies and feelings, which we look upon as a nation. The United States will one day be the same.

Seꭺ.—But what are these feelings? Define them? "Feeling" is a most indefinite word.

Ꭺꞃꞇ.—There you have me. I haven't studied philosophy, I can see their effects, but I can't describe them.

Seꭺ.—So you break down, too. You'll have to give in to my view.

Seu.—Certainly not, for my part. The more we argue the more I feel convinced that there exists a real thing called a nation—not a mere name; and that Ireland is a nation in that sense. *We* may not be able to define or prove it, yet, somehow, I know it to be real.

ᴀᴘᴄ.—Just my feelings (I beg your pardon for using the word). We'll never give in. But are we any longer in agreement as to the Irish language?

Seᴀ.—Of course it's necessary to my special "Irish nationality." You two chaps oughtn't to wait for the second part of the concert. You've both said language is not essential.

Seu.—Theoretically, perhaps. But with English literature and thought pouring in on us, I'm afraid, in practice, my "sum total" would soon come down to nothing if we had not got our language as a preservative. It is the one really distinctive thing we have, and it's worth all the rest put together.

ᴀᴘᴄ.—My "community of feeling" would soon follow.

Seᴀ.—So then we are all agreed on one thing, that the Irish language is, in practice, necessary to our nationality.

Seu.—We can, therefore, listen to Part II. with easy consciences.

ᴀᴘᴄ.—Even intervals can improve the mind.

(At this point the Band struck up *A Nation Once Again.*)

IV.—Looking beyond England.

THERE must be two factors in the development of every nation. That which it evolves out of itself, the product of its own organic growth, and that which it derives from outside. We may develop our lives and our institutions ourselves, or we may follow the perilous but often necessary course of adopting ready-made, the highly-developed product of another country's mind. We may, for instance, to take a simple example, either develop a native

literature of our own, or, as the Romans did,
adopt the developed literature of some other nation,
as it lies ready to hand, whether by translating
its masterpieces or by merely absorbing its images
and root ideas. In the case of a country such
as our own, where development has been artificially
arrested for so long a period, there is a very
serious problem involved in deciding between the two
methods. It is by no means easy to say where precisely we should draw the line between organic
development and the absorption of outside matter,
how far we should be satisfied with homespun, and
how far we should seek to clothe ourselves in
foreign fabrics of delicate texture. The question is
one that must receive a practical solution according
to the facts of each particular case. It is one to
which no general answer is possible.

In the present article I only speak of that class
of cases where the question has been decided, and
decided in favour of adoption. In some matters, as
for instance, in mechanics, any other conclusion would
be sheer lunacy. No one would propose, for example,
that Messrs. Pierce should refuse to adopt the invention of the "free wheel," and wait till our national
genius had devised some more characteristic but
equally pleasant method of descending inclines. In
other matters, such as language, to decide to adopt
the product of the foreigner should equally be regarded as lunacy in the opposite direction. That in this
country it is not, is due to the fact that the Irishman
who advises such a course is—in the phrase of a
foreign poet—"mad in the customary way." The
numbers of the mentally afflicted secure them universal
respect.

In some matters, then, we must seek aid from
abroad, we must adopt what we cannot conveniently
evolve. Where are we to seek such aid? Whence
shall our adoptions be derived? Hitherto the question has only received one answer, "England." Praise

of England is not popular amongst us.   One form of
flattery of that country is, however, very much in
vogue.   We are ever ready to pay it the meed of
imitation.   Our literature, our drama, our institutions,
our law, and our social life, we draw one and all from
an English source.   Much of these we might develop
for ourselves, though some we must needs import.
An original literature, for instance, we may very well
hope for.   A wholly original Irish philosophy could,
at this date, scarcely be produced.

But if we must import philosophy, or anything
else, why should we confine our researches to Britain?
Why should we be satisfied to derive our stock of
universal ideas from the second-rate philosophy of
modern England, the shallow evolutionary creed of
Herbert Spencer and his followers?   Why should we
not call the whole world to our assistance, and, going
to the true fountain-head of philosophy, to Aristotle
or to St. Thomas, and for certain purposes to the
philosophers of Germany, seek to adopt ideas which
shall be far ahead of those of our neighbours.   The vast
mass of current English thought, whether scientific or
literary, is at once shallow and opposed to Catholic
teaching.   Yet whenever we have to go outside of
Irish writings, we are content to accept the poor and
pernicious product of the English mind ; we never
dream of going beyond England and seeking com-
munion with European culture, and as a result the
Catholic literature of the world is a sealed book to
us.

But this is not a consideration peculiar to philosophy.   It is of far wider extension.   Above all we
look to England for "standards."   Suppose some
social question is being discussed, some new scheme
of municipal enterprise; or, again, say such a matter
as the admission of women into another profession.
What is the one enquiry made, the only test put forward, " What have they done in England ?"   The
rest of the civilised world, where, perhaps, we should

find many examples of circumstances more like our own, is completely blotted out from view. France, Germany, Russia, even America are left out of sight. "What they do in England" decides everything. So with Irish workmen and Irish manufacturers. England is taken as the only standard for comparison, the sole object of imitation. The workman of Ireland demands that he shall be assimilated to his brother in England. His employer who refuses his demand, is himself equally determined to put before him the methods of the English manufacturer as the highest point of his endeavour. Any thought of accepting other models, and getting ahead of England, never occurs to either.

The destructive effects of this narrowness of view are sufficiently apparent. Much silly legislation, many economic mistakes, a great number of harmful social conventions have been its results. It may be interesting to note a few instances in which a more sensible course has been adopted, in which a thorough examination of Irish needs has been combined with an investigation of the methods by which similar needs are dealt with in the rest of Europe. The system of co-operative societies was formed entirely on a continental model, since native selfishness made them impossible in England. Again, the system of bringing about a peasant proprietory by land purchase, one of the few legislative schemes which has been an admitted success as far as it went—I am not discussing the recent measure and the questions which it raises—was largely of Continental origin. The Dublin tram-system too, was entirely copied from the system of a continental city. These are a few examples of the value of not confining ourselves to England when we are obliged to go outside of Ireland. I do not advocate undue cosmopolitanism. We should develop on our own lines as far as possible. But when we do find it necessary to look beyond our own country, we should take as wide a survey as possible.

V. —After the Abbey is Over.

F. McCumhail
  A Queen } *á la* Yeats.

Michael Donovan
Mary Henessy } *á la* Gregory.

M. D.—Faith, and it's little we'd be understandin'
  you, then, and us hearin' ye so often.

F. McC.—For out—of the land of—shadows, out of
  the kingdom of dreams I wandered—a prince—
  of red-golden fame.

M. H.—Is it fame that's on you now? Sure and it's
  mighty few that do be seeing you, withal,
  Francis McCool.

F. McC.—Yea—for their eyes—are the eyes of men.
  But—I am famed—among the undying gods—
  the purple gods that dwell in the ashen clouds.

M. D.—Sure there isn't any "gods," and not many
  in the gallery neether, save of a Sathurde.

F. McC.—You see not. For you—are begotten—
  of a woman's love—but I am of a rainbow,
  liquid lovely—by a king, a king that was be-
  guiled—by fleeting seemliness of cloudy form.

M. D.—Faith, I'm thinkin', Mary Henessy, it's after
  the father he takes, more th'n the mother.

M. H.—Indeed, it's little wonder his father'd be
  lovin' a rainbow, Michael Donovan, and he
  so black. I do see the poor man trippin'
  up and down them stairs every mortal night.

M. D.—But I never heard tell it was a rainbow he
  was afther neether, Mary Henessy.

F. McC.—Nay, there shall be no after, but everything—always ever—and forever, dream upon
  dream.

B

M. D.—He manes that they'll be always puttin' him on first, Mary Henessy.

M. H.—Sure, God help the poor creatur', none o' them that come here'd be mindin' him at all if they didn't ; and he so distraught. God forgive me.

F. McC.—For—I—am a king's son—and a king's son shall ever be first—at the feast.

M. H.—Then it's a cold feast would be at you, Francis McCool, I'm thinkin', without us bein' here

F. McC.—For you—are the children of men—and the taste of kingly speech—is not—upon your lips.

M. D.—It's a mighty poor taste, entirely, then without you'd be havin' somethin' more to eat, these times.

M. H.—That's true for ye, Michael Donovan, but sure the poor gentleman doesn't undersand.

F. McC.—The taste of kingly speech and scent of kingly dream, of chrysolite—dissolved in nectar —web of golden thought—and woof of love— acanthus blossom dropping on a sombre wave.

(Enter a Queen).

Q.—Beloved, oh, soul—oh, crowned child of beauty, many-hued, begot of her—that was begotten of the sadness of the dawn—or of the hope of sunset, having for a life but nature's mood, a mood divine, yet tinged with death. Son of the dew—that glistens on a rose-leaf in the light, the mystic answer to the golden beam—or changing colour—of the shimmering pearl upon a mirror's edge.

F. McC.—Sweet love—the golden mistletoe that nestles on the shady bough—the haze that shapes the distant hill into a mystic form—the tide—that laps upon the silver shore—the flight of swallows—rising to the sun.

Q.—Oh, deathless love, I see the birds.

F. McC.—I hear the dirge-sweet music in the air.

M. D.—Sure they 're well matched, Mary Henessy.

M. H.—I am thinkin' she 'd be kin to the dark man, likewise.

M. D.—Maybe she would, now, and her talkin' like that. There don't be many reared that way, now-a-days.

M. H.—Sure they were all reared that way, oncest I 'm tould, Michael Donovan.

M. D.—And she to be the daughter of a king.

M. H.—To think of her lodgin' with the likes of us.

M. D.—Sure you 'd be hard set, then, to find a meal or a lodgin' in Dublin many a time, and the people so hard to please. I 'm thinkin' they 're glad enough to share in the bit and sup we bring in of a night and they talkin' of livin' on rainbows. And we're betther company than the lad that come fr'm out the West whether or no, him that bate his father.

M. H.—Sure it's little we grudge what they eat, and they such genteel folk accustomed t' all kinds of splendour.

M. D.—Maybe they 'd see betther days agen, if they gave up dhramin'.

M. H.—Sure we're all as God made us.

------◆------

VI.—Art and Nationality.

WE are beginning to take an interest in the subject of Art. It is a symptom of the national awakening. The Irish movement extends into many fields, and this demand for the life artistic, which is now beginning to make itself felt, is only a new application of the cry, " More life,"

which is essentially the call of our national revival.
Yet, at first sight, this matter of art is beyond all else
disappointing.   Art is, perhaps, at a lower ebb
amongst ourselves than amongst any other civilized
nation.   To say that we are an artistic people, if we
confine the word to its ordinary and narrower meaning which refers to pictorial art, is to make an empty
boast, which must straightaway be contradicted by
facts.   For such a claim is own brother to the fable
that Dublin is a musical city.   Velasquez has fewer
admirers amongst us than Beethoven.   Nor does the
outlook seem particularly promising.

Again it may seem carping, but I venture to question whether most modern Irish pictures *are* Irish art.
Are they not rather Anglo-Irish art?   To the ordinary
man—and I do not claim to any loftier critical
eminence—it is impossible to perceive any well-
marked distinction between modern Irish and English
pictures.   The Irishmen are second-class Romneys
and third-class Reynolds's.   Their pictures are painted,
as it were, in the language of English art.   There is
none of that national individuality which at once
distinguishes French pictures.   Anyone could tell
that a Greuze was not the work of an Englishman, even if he did not know its authorship, or
the special manner of its creator.   Who could say
this much of Irish painters?   They paint in the
English way, to suit a taste formed on English
models, and they can in no way be considered
as reflecting the life, thoughts, or feelings of their
native country.

In truth though the circumstances in some cases
differ, the problem of an Irish artistic revival, like
that of a literary and a musical revival, must find its
solution, if it is ever to find one, through the medium
of nationality.   In the case of literature this has been
fully, and in the case of music partially, recognised.
And the case of art is essentially similar.   In all three
instances we are confronted with native arts (in the wider
sense) which have reached a certain stage of develop-

ment and stopped short. The rest of the world has meantime progressed. Our problem is to take the elements contained in the partially developed native art, and making use of foreign exemplars, bring them up to the stage of complete development. In the case of literature, this is comparatively easy. The development of this form of art, the one most closely connected with our lives, has never entirely ceased. So in music the task is by no means impossible. Esposito and Hamilton Harty have shown us what can be done by the use of our simple Irish airs as the themes for a more elaborate composition. The difficulty of developing a true national art is, however, extremely great, by reason of the fact that amongst us art has scarcely had any large development at all.

The beginnings of art are, to some extent, formless. Our sense of beauty first manifests itself in ornament. Architecture comes next. The use of the human form as an element in artistic representation comes late. Painting is the last of all to attain full development and side by side with this development of art goes a development of artistic taste. It is our misfortune that, as a nation, and expressing ourselves in terms of our national ideas, we have never progressed beyond the first stage of ornamentation, and a partial progress in the second, architecture. All the rest has been imported. The national mind has hitherto found no expression in higher art, and it in great part explains why any desire or taste for high art is wholly absent among us. As a nation our artistic appreciation has remained equally undeveloped, and if you seek the explanation why an Italian gloats over a picture to which an Irishman can scarce afford a glance, the true reason is that as a nation a true sense of artistic form has not yet come into being among us.

But what remedy is there for our deficiencies? The answer is not easy. It is clear that we can never truly develop any but a national art and a national taste for it—cosmopolitan art is a mere occasional monstrosity—but it is by no means equally

apparent *how* we are to develop it. For in the
matter of art there is a very special difficulty. An
art gallery and an art school may develop artists.
In both we may properly make use of foreign
models, to help in the development of our national
art, just as Reubens, though a Fleming, drew much
from the Italians. And Mr. Hugh Lane is doing a very
good work in this direction. But who is to feed your
artist when you get him. For there are no Civil Service
examinations for art students. The Dublin Corporation has been suggested—and it has given money
for an art gallery — but the rates are already
about ten shillings in the pound. " No industry, no
anything," is again the stumbling-block. Artists
must always be the dependents of the wealthy classes.
And one need not dilate on the smallness of the assistance we can get from the Irish aristocracy in any
national development; as things are at present,
there is very little hope in that direction. I can,
indeed, see only one field in which a national art,
pictorial or statuesque, may be developed.

Much has been written on the subject of eccle-
siastical art. Might not a national religious art be
produced in Ireland ? Greek art was almost wholly
religious. It flourished in a country where private
dwelling-houses were poor and unadorned, and individual sumptuousness almost unknown. And in such
art the artist is peculiarly the servant of the many and
not of the few. Now Religion is that which, above all
else, is dear to Irishmen. All our conceptions of beauty,
all our highest ideals are bound up with it. Why
should we not, like the Flemish, have a native
religious art, and not confine our efforts in this
direction to German reproductions of Italian originals ? Why should we not, as at Bruges, have
Madonnas and Apostles, whose features were the
idealisation of Irish faces, a loveliness fresh with
the breath of our own life, and not a halting
copy of some dead foreign imagining. In Ireland
there is still faith, the soul of art. Could not the

love of formless beauty at present characteristic of
the nation be thus made to take material shape
in religious representation. With happier conditions, other forms of art might follow later. But a
religious art would be a splendid commencement.
And if there is to be a true development of Irish
art at all, this seems to be the one avenue open
to it, under present conditions.

VII.—The Revival of the English Language.

(*Translated from* " An neiṁ-ṗleaḃac," beiḃḟeiḟḟṫe, 199—, A.D.)

THE report which we publish in another column
of the meeting held yesterday in the capital
of Ulster will be read with interest by our
readers. Whilst such an important question as that
of taxation reform remains unsettled, we think that
other matters can well afford to wait; yet the pro-
moters of this meeting have, no doubt, a deserving,
if somewhat impracticable object in view, and they
will command the sympathy of many who may not
be prepared to go the whole way with them in their
aspirations.

.   .   .   .

REPORT.

A meeting was held yesterday at the Custom
House, under the presidency of the Lord Mayor, who
is himself an English speaker. Many members of
the licensed trade were present. His lordship said
that he congratulated them on the vast assemblage
that was here present to-day (prolonged applause).
Politics had not lessened his enthusiasm for his
native tongue. Ulster would speak with no un-
certain voice in this matter (loud cheers).

The Rev. Nathaniel Trew then addressed the

meeting. His reference to the hallowed and historic nature of the ground on which they stood evoked great enthusiasm. His sainted ancestor had once stood upon these steps. Here he had spoken words of wisdom in the English tongue. If that great man were now to address them, how few, alas, would understand him. Yet, scarce a hundred years since, he had striven in friendly rivalry with the ancestor of Lord Mayor Sloane. He would, however, avoid politics. The Irish language was gradually sapping their spirit. Their intercourse with England (cheers) had ceased ; the Saxon was becoming the prey of the Gael. Only the other day a venal Viceroy had addressed Parliament in Irish. He had already delayed them too long (No, no). He would conclude with the English phrase, "Buck-up." Let it be their motto. (A man who called out " ꞁᴀꞮméꞮꞁ" at this point was instantly ejected.)

Lord M'Connell of Antrim said that the movement had his cordial support. The English language might not be musical, yet all systems of music were not the same. The Chinese and the Indian system differed from our own. The language was at any rate forcible. Who could read the speeches of the Lord Mayor's ancestor or the contemporary poems of Kipling—*magnum et venerabile nomen*—(a voice— "Down with Rome"), without perceiving in them a virile eloquence which the Irish could never hope to attain. He suggested that they should place the movement under the patronage of his Majesty. Personally he would subscribe £1 (tremendous applause).

Alderman Saunderson heartily thanked his lordship for his more than kind words of encouragement . and his generous donation. He himself was entitled to speak as a commercial man. Though Esperanto had now been adopted as the language of commerce, English had once been regarded as eminently suited for business purposes. American was merely a dialect of English, and one with a knowledge of written

English could pick it up in a few months. Though it was not strictly revelant to their meeting to-day, he hoped they would also interest themselves in the question of the repeal of the Prohibition laws (loud cheers).

Sir John Mahaffy-Pentland, D.C.L., of Dublin, said he wished to address himself to the practical side of the question. His family had always supported the language. Had Trinity College maintained its independence, loyalty and language would never have been undermined. They might learn lessons from their oppressor (loud hissing). The Gaelic League (much booing) had sprung from small beginnings. In these days a man need not conceal his sentiments (hear, hear). Amidst great enthusiasm he quoted a passage from the writings of Provost Mahaffy (cheers), in which he stigmatised ancient Irish literature as either silly or immoral.

A *soirée*, which corresponds to a ɼᵹoᴘuɩᴅeᴀċᴛ, was then held. The ancient English air, "God Save the King," was received with much interest and applause.

Several of the other airs rendered seemed to lack volume. The traditional English airs, "Bloime she's 'is a donah" (modernised "Bless me, she is his *fiancée*"), and "Loo-oo, dat's 'oo, dat's oo" (It's yourself, Louisa"), were, however, especially interesting, though the banjo accompaniment scarcely accords with modern musical ideas.

After many other items the meeting separated amid great enthusiasm, singing "ᴮuᴀɩᴸ ᴀn Pᴀᴘᴀ" and "ᴛɩɼᵹe nᴀ ᴮoɩnne."

VIII.—The Commercial Value of Patriotism.

THE cynic will smile at this title. He will rejoice to hear that the "patriot" industry is receiving public recognition, that the monetary aspects of "patriotism," at which he has often hinted, are at last being taken into account as commercial assets. But no reference is intended to the advantage individuals may or may not derive from politics, for I speak of patriotism without inverted commas. And although true patriotism often benefits him that has it materially as well as morally and intellectually, yet it is of the benefit which results to a com- munity as a whole from a wide-spread love of country that I wish to treat.

It was in a conversation with an old friend and fellow-student that these reflections occurred to me. We were discussing the possibility (in the circumstances a likely one) of his having the choice of two positions of nearly equal value, the one in London, the other in Ireland. In such a case he said he would undoubtedly choose the London one. He was a man on whose education several hundred pounds had been spent, not a little of it public money. And now, at the first opportunity, he was ready to leave the country. Only a few days afterwards I was speaking to another, a young man beginning his student course, the son of a well- known public-spirited Irishman.* We fell to talk of his future. " Of course, I am not a home-bird," he said, with a laugh, " I have no objection to emigrat- ing." Neither of these were exceptional in their views. I know of many another who has held the same opinions and put them into practice on the earliest possible occasion.

When you find such an attitude of mind, even in young men, you cannot but think that there must be something wrong in the system of education that has produced them. And that there is something wrong we already know as a fact. We are all aware of the want of patriotism and nationality that disgraces so many of our schools, and is a natural result of our educational system. Yet it does not come home to everyone what the results of this want of patriotism are. That emigration is too often a direct outcome of Scholastic West-Britainism, is a truth that we do

* He has in fact since left for a foreign country.

not all immediately appreciate. Men are indifferent as to how their children are brought up, and they do not realise that one result of their indifference is that great loss of money and money's worth which is involved in the dread malady of depopulation. The spread of education has often been pointed to as the chief source of a nation's prosperity. But in Ireland the very spread of education defeats itself. For as there is no leaven of patriotism in our instruction, a man is no sooner educated than he leaves the country, and all the money that has been spent on his upbringing proves to be so much loss of national capital.

There is unhappily, an idea current in Ireland that there is an antagonism between patriotism and prosperity. Undoubtedly in the case of individuals, some countenance is lent to the notion by the too frequent opportunities which in this country the unpatriotic have for feathering their nests. Moreover, owing to historical causes, most of the fatness of the land is in the hands of men of anti-Irish sentiment. It is this fact which leads to a certain contempt for any patriotic element in education. Anything of the sort is considered *unpractical.* Why should a *commercial* training concern itself with things Irish ? What has sentiment of that sort got to do with the everyday business of the world ? Men fail to recognise that the inculcation of patriotism is even more vital to the well-being of a country than the spread of literary education or technical instruction. The latter help to furnish the national edifice, or to make life pleasant and wholesome within it, but patriotism is the mortar that holds the walls together ; and without it all other adornment and improvement is in vain ; the structure must eventually become a ruin.

The material advantages of patriotism to a people are manifold, and we can without difficulty estimate them in this country by our familiarity with their contraries. Not only does patriotism diminish emigration, but it creates a public spirit in those who remain. The

country is not looked on as a common prey. Public
functions are carried on with some view to the
public welfare rather than to the comfort and
aggrandisement of individuals. Legislation like
government tends to become far sighted and benefi-
cent, for as the government is concerned for the
welfare of the people, the people do not regard
it as the common enemy. In other countries such
truths as these have become the platitudes of everyday experience. In Ireland they are but the aspirations of the Ivory Gate—the only door that is open
to its unhappy inhabitants.

What again is better calculated to create and
foster a distinctive national art? And such an art is of
immense value to industry; for the development of
high art brings about the development of applied
arts as a natural consequence. Even in the direction of science and mechanical invention, patriotism
has its value. Once the country is looked on as truly
a country, an emulation is likely to spring up
between the scientists within its borders, and a
school of native science and invention will probably
result therefrom. The isolated workers, with nothing
to spur them on, with whom we are at present
familiar in Ireland, produce but disappointing results.

Germany is the country where the spirit of nationality is strongest. Patriotism is there more intense
than among any other people. Yet it is but of recent
growth and has developed in less than a century. Is
it found inconsistent with commercial prosperity? On
the contrary there is no people whose manufactures
are more prosperous. Scientific training and technical education have been brought, as we know, to a
higher degree of perfection there than anywhere else.
Art, literature, and music all alike flourish. And it
is the spirit of patriotism that has done all this.
Though the Germans are more bound up in themselves than any other nation ; yet they are none the
less the best-informed about the affairs and circum-

stances of other countries. Profoundly devoted to their own language, they are amongst the best instructed in foreign tongues. The most attached to ideals, they are yet the most careful of the practical affairs of life of any people in Europe. A broad and rational patriotism has added material success to national unity.

What is true of the Germans, is true in a slightly lesser degree of all the prosperous peoples in the world. The Frenchman, the Italian, the Magyar, the Czech, have all alike founded prosperity on love of country. It is only amongst a people similarly circumstanced as ourselves that a cynical disregard of public obligations is looked on as the true path to success. Ireland is about the only country in the world where patriot is used as a term of reproach. It is only amongst ourselves that such a view of life, would be permitted to be actively or, at any rate tacitly inculcated in schools supported by public money. Does a single patriotic sentiment form part of the ordinary educational course of an Irish boy. Personally I never met any such. Though I do not refer to what an individual teacher may himself add outside the prescribed curriculum. If, then, we are eager to spread education among our people, let it be true education, and have in it the leaven of patriotism, for if it have not, it is a deadly food and contains within it the seeds of dissolution.

IX.—Going to Trinity.

Mrs. X.—Really, James, he must go to Trinity.

Dr. X.—I don't think, my dear, it would be advisable for us to take such a step at present.

Mrs. X.—But why shouldn't he ? Isn't he quite as clever as Mrs. Brown's sons. Our Georgie shouldn't be at any disadvantage.

Dr. X.—Of course not, my dear, but Mrs. Brown is different.

Mrs. X.—Very different, indeed, her father was a ——

Dr. X.—A very honest and decent man.

Mrs. X.—They always *are* honest. If Brown had not married her for her money——

Dr. X.—She might have been sending her sons to the Catholic University.

Mrs. X.—It would have been the proper place for them, where they would meet their equals. But that is no reason why my son should go there.

Dr. X.—But you see, my dear——

Mrs. X.—I don't see.

Dr. X.—As to an English school. I did not mind.

Mrs. X.—You ought to be very glad I insisted on it.

Dr. X.—Of course from the point of view of religion, that was all right.

Mrs. X.—Of course.

Dr. X.—And if it were Oxford.

Mrs. X.—Oh, I do wish you could send him there. Jack Murphy got a scholarship, or exhibition, or something of £80 a year, and Georgie might do the same.

Dr. X.—Well, I asked them at the school, and they said it was only very clever boys ——

Mrs. X.—But he *is* very clever, James.

Dr. X.—Clever at *examinations*, that had any chance, and of course I can't afford £200 or £300 a year, with Lilly's presentation and all these other expenses.

Mrs. X.—Then, James, that proves what I said already. You must send him to Trinity.

Dr. X.—But then, my dear, there is the religious difficulty.

Mrs. X.—Really, James, you are not generally so pious. It was as much as I could do to get you to come to Mass when we were at Eastbourne.

Dr. X.—I don't mean religious in that sense. You see this is a public matter.

Mrs. X.—What can it matter to other people how we educate our children.

Dr. X.—But you see other Catholics.

Mrs. X.—There are Catholics and Catholics.

Dr. X.—Other Catholics might follow our example, we would be giving scandal.

Mrs. X.—I think you ought to see, James, this absurd parade of religion is very much out of place.

Dr. X.—But hang it all, Marie, I can't afford to make enemies at present. There might be a paragraph about it in ——.

Mrs. X.—No respectable people read it.

Dr. X.—But the clergy read it.

Mrs. X.—O, James, he must go !

Dr. X.—Well, I say he shan't. Not just yet, anyhow. (A ring. Servant enters with card. Dr. X. reads.) Mr. Alfonsus Supple. That awful bore ! (Advancing)—Ah, my dear Supple, won't you come in? Marie, this is Mr. Supple.

Mrs. X.—Mr. Supple has just come at the right time, we are talking about education.

Mr. Supple.—Always my pet hobby, Mrs. X.

Mrs. X.—Now do you think, Mr. Supple, we should be justified ——

Dr. X.—O, Marie, I don't think we ought to bore poor Mr. Supple with our domestic difficulties, he is very hard-worked just at present.

Mr. Supple.—Oh, if it 's about education, I am sure I shall be most interested ; are you sending another boy to Hurstside ?

Dr. X.—Oh, no, it 's still about Georgie. You see, Supple, my wife was wanting me to send him to Trinity. But I told her I did not think College quite a fit place —— Of course, there are grave dangers.

Mrs. X.—Indeed, you never said anything of the sort, James.

THE IDEA OF A NATION.

Mr. Supple.—I had to face them myself.

Mrs. X.—Oh, we know you were *very* distinguished, Mr. Supple.

Mr. Supple.—But still one may take precautions. When a boy has been trained at Hurstside ——.

Mrs. X.—There now, James, I knew Mr. Supple would agree with me, and Mr. Supple is the Secretary of the Catholic Committee.

Mr. Supple.—" The Catholic Gentry's Protest Committee;" indeed, it was about that I came. I want to induce your husband to second a resolution on Friday. You see here is the paper.

Dr. X. (reads)—" That we protest in the most solemn manner against the intolerable wrong ——" (hum). Oh, I ought to be able to say a few words on that.

Mrs. X.—And I'll go to hear him. Won't you get me a ticket, Mr. Supple?

Mr. Supple.—Of course, Mrs. X; but you'll have to to come early now that we've got Dr. X to speak.

Dr. X.—But about this matter, Supple, do you really think it would be quite consistent for me to send my son to Trinity. Wouldn't it look rather like flying in the face of the Bishops' Resolution?

Mr. S.—Oh, no. That is only a general prohibition. Of course, if any individual who has been well grounded in his faith feels himself strong enough he is at perfect liberty to use his own judgment.

Mrs. X.—So Georgie may go, mayn't he?

Mr. S.—I am sure there couldn't possibly be a clearer case.

Mrs. X.—And you'll let him, won't you, hubbie?

Dr. X.—Well, when both you and Mr. Supple agree, I don't think I'll be able to hold out, and now, Supple, you must stay for tea.

Mr. S.—Oh, not for the world. I have to get to the committee meeting at once. But you won't forget Friday night. We'll shake the Government up !

Dr. X.—Oh, I'll be there. I see you're not afraid of colds ! *Au revoir.*

------◆------

X.—Nationality and Music.

THE merits and demerits of the Feis Ceoil have been fully and candidly discussed ; a detailed consideration has been given to its several items by trained musicians. I cannot hope, nor do I desire, to follow their footsteps. I cannot hope to estimate the feast from the same point of view as an expert in musical gastronomy. Of the banquet of harmony I can only speak from the position of a humble diner-out, who can perceive that the fare is good, but is not always capable of truly appreciating the subtle flavours of *Consommé d'Allegretto,* and *Potage à l'Andante.* I only venture to treat of our musical festival from an ordinary point of view.

The Feis Ceoil is a strange mixture to the Irish Irelander. He is never entirely content and never entirely dissatisfied with it. He is about to denounce it as too cosmopolitan when it bursts forth into some glorious Irish melody. He is beginning to consider it Irish when he meets with some of those many un-Irish features to which allusion has frequently been made. It is indeed to some extent a compromise between wealthy, respectable, un-Irish music-lovers and poor, talented, Gaelic-loving Irishmen. Perhaps it is the best that can be devised. It might be hard to get on without the monetary support of the former, and it is for want of the personal support of the latter, that so many musical undertakings in this country have perished of inanition.

We are all tolerably familiar with musical and

C

artistic movements in Ireland. They are started, as
a rule, by a few cultured persons, who are wholly out
of touch with Irish feeling, and, for the most part,
lead lives of wasted and barren intellectuality.
Many others join the undertaking for social reasons.
Distinguished persons attend the first beginnings of
the new creation, and a crowded audience assembles
to greet the distinguished orchestra. The novelty
soon wears off. It ceases to be fashionable and the
guarantors are called on to pay the creditors. There
may be some countries where exotic art can flourish.
But in Ireland it must be of the nation or not
at all.

As the Irish Nation has but just now awoken
to the consciousness of its existence, so it is but just
beginning to realise the necessity of expressing that
existence in artistic forms. We may not all be
capable of appreciating the highest art, but expressly
or implicitly, in our social as well as in our intellectual life, we have the desire for Irish art. The
Gaelic League has sought to fulfil that desire in
many directions. The Feis Ceoil has also, to some
extent, supplied it, and to this is due such share of
success as it has attained. The most beautiful
original item I have ever heard at a Feis Ceoil was,
to my mind, Hardebeck's "Lament of Deirdre,"
as sung in Gaelic by J. C. Doyle some years ago.
Its success was enormous. Those in the dearer
seats received it languidly. But the body of the
audience demanded and finally compelled an aꞃíꞃ.
For men felt that it was not mere barren art. It
was Ireland once again voicing itself in song.

In music, however, a problem which I have mentioned in a previous essay meets us in a concrete
form. How far should we seek to develop national pro-
ducts, and to what extent should we adopt the best
product of the foreigner? We have much beautiful
music of our own of a simple melodic form. The
more developed complex forms we have not. And
the question of precisely how far we should import

the music of other countries is a very difficult one.
Many people will probably think the Feis Ceoil
in some respects adopts too much. It should, above
all, keep from imposing English music upon us. For
even where we lack musical types of our own, we have
no need for the soulless productions of a second-rate
musical nation. In treating of importations it should,
however, be remembered that an importation may substantially be naturalised. The music of Handel, for
instance, though ferociously denounced by contemporary English writers has now become incorporated
into English life, and is practically English music.
In some directions we might also naturalise foreign
art with advantage. Still another question, however
—the reflexion in music of a well-known problem
in literature—is how far the work of an Irish com-
poser is always to be considered Irish. How far is
music to be considered Irish that does not partake of
the distinctive characteristics of our ancient music.
I do not here touch on the vexed question of
Traditionalism, though I should gladly see anything
distinctive in our musical heritage preserved and
developed. Of course, in any form of art we might
develop a style, which would very greatly depart from
the ancient style and yet be characteristically national.
Mascagni and Leoncavallo, and the modern school
of Italian composers, for instance, have developed a
school which, though essentially Italian, yet is in
great measure founded on German music, and departs
very widely from the traditional style of musical
composition in Italy, though as to its value there have
been different opinions. Might we not expect something of the same kind in Ireland? In considering such
questions, however, we must never forget that our
nationality is at present in a very much weaker condition than that of England or of Italy, and hence
we might find a process of assimilation in many
matters both difficult and dangerous. Whatever
course we adopt, however, Nationhood must ever
be the vivifying principle and final end of the move-

ment. There is no longer any place for unattached
cosmopolitan art in Ireland.

But, in truth, modern Irish music remains·to be
written. There is a mine of virgin gold ready for
them that will work it. Our ancestors have handed
down to us two precious possessions. A mythology
of marvellous beauty, far different from the mon-
strous absurdities with which Wagner had to cope;
and side by side with it a body of melody, of
infinite variety and exquisite loveliness. What our
own age has to do is to fuse them together, and
tell our story in terms of our Art; to weave the
beautiful themes that are our traditional heritage,
the golden thread of song, into a delicate complex
fabric that shall limb the legends of Finn and
Cuchulain. To combine our subtly simply beautiful
airs into the wonderful complex forms of advanced
modern music. Nor is, perhaps, the making of the
golden thread itself yet a lost art.

When modern Irish music shall have been
achieved, it will have a style all its own, lovely,
hallowed, distant, beautiful; a splendid purple
beauty of hope ever tinged with sad, subtle melancholy. It will portray the passion of the soul, not of
the senses, a striving for the sublime ideal. Tir-na-
nog will be to it as the holy Grail. It will seek the
unknowable amid the thrill of the violin and the
sacred note of the harp. It will differ by all the
world from Carmen, or Cavalleria, or Traviata.
The wild, mad rush of overpowering passion will
be foreign to it. For of all the direful strivings of
man, there will remain to it only the sad shadow
of sorrow. I speak not of all Irish music. We shall
still have jigs and dances, and tales of love and war.
But if there shall, as I hope, arise among us great
masters, grand architects of sound, it is in this wise
they shall build their fairy palace as a home for Eire,
the undying queen.

XI.—Nationality and Culture.

CULTURE is a word of somewhat indefinite meaning. It is sometimes used as denoting little more than mere conventional politeness, a familiarity with the arbitrary habits which custom has made law among the higher classes of society. Both culture and education are often misused in such a sense. And it is as a result of this usage that we often hear Catholic priests spoken of as uncultivated and uneducated by those who are in reality infinitely inferior to them both in culture and education. With such critics a deep acquaintance with philosophy, or a real knowledge and appreciation of poetry, weighs as little, compared with the science of afternoon-calling or the knowledge of the correct method of helping round tea. But Culture in its true sense is a far different thing. It denotes the complete development of oneself and one's faculties. And if it has come to have any connection with the freemasonry and symbolism of "high life" it is merely because the leisured classes have, as a rule, greater opportunities of mental cultivation, opportunities, however, that are by no means invariably availed of.

Culture being the complete development of a man, it is after spiritual duties and the necessary work of our position in life, the highest end to which we can devote ourselves, and it is even in some measure enjoined upon us by a spiritual sanction. It has then seemed to some a very grave objection to the movement for Irish Nationhood that it appeared to involve an opposition to culture, a turning away from intellectual ideas. I have often heard arguments of this nature, not always, indeed, clearly formulated, urged against the policy of the Gaelic

League. And they have, no doubt, a certain apparent truth in them. The movement for Irish Nationality does invite us to shut off not a few of what have hitherto been the channels through which we have derived intellectual life. Its trend is opposed to the literature, the music and the art, which have hitherto been current in Ireland. It looks with disfavour on the theatre, with which we are familiar. And it bids us put from us much of what we have hitherto regarded as our main intellectual food. Cursorily examined it seems to involve almost a worse iconoclasm than the early forms of English puritanism.

Of course this statement of the demands of the Irish movement is exaggerated. For it is rather English degradation than English culture that it combats. As to the latter it does not demand that we should wholly banish it, any more than the culture of any other nation; it only requires that we should not steep ourselves in it or give ourselves wholly up to it, as has hitherto been the case. And it is because the channels of intellectual life in this country have been so far monopolised by things English, that a movement for nationality falsely seems to connote a movement against intellectuality. No view could be more mistaken. For in reality nothing is more favourable to intellectuality than the Irish movement. It is not the theatre, but the English theatre, and not so much the English theatre as the more degraded forms of it that the Irish movement condemns. So it is not music, but English music, and not so much English music as the most inane and debased types of it that it has found it necessary to censure.

There is, no doubt, a certain initial wrench. There is the uncertainty and displeasure of a change. Our small Irish home is not always as sumptuously furnished as our former luxurious and gaudy apartments in the palatial English hotel. But it is to ultimate results that we must have regard; and, judged by that standard, it is clear that in the long run the Irish movement involves a culture more real, more deeply rooted, more widely spread than anything we have ever obtained from England. Not a little of seeming English culture is superficial. Its popular philosophy is shallow, its popular music empty tunefulness, its popular art without idea or purpose. It is this superficial culture that has hitherto been most readily assimilated in Ireland, the philosophy of Herbert Spencer, the music of Stephen Adams. And it is such poor stuff that the Irish movement would sweep away. Of what is real and good in English life we have assimilated very little.

But the Irish movement is not merely a negative one. No doubt there will be found extremists, whose doctrines are so narrow that they give ground for such a statement. This, however, is the fate of every movement for good, and as theologians tell us of some of the saints, we should rather admire their devotion than seek to imitate their manifestations of it. The Irish movement is really a great constructive movement. It seeks to develop a many-sided culture, a wide and far-reaching intellectuality, which shall have its mainspring in nationality. And has it not largely succeeded in its endeavour ? Have not its fruits in literature and music been ample ? How many people are now beginning to have a sense of what true music is, and an appreciation of poetic beauty, who previously were repelled or stultified by the sterile compositions of modern *bourgeois* England and Anglo-Ireland.

But, above all, what an intellectual awakening there has been amongst those whom the Irish movement has touched. How many who, up to this, had no thought above the everyday things of life have had their minds aroused to a true and healthy culture by its teachings. Not a few, indeed, have become champions of the Gaelic League because of this fact alone, who might perhaps have been opposed to it on its intrinsic merits. The intellectual awakening of the Irish movement has always seemed

to me very like the intellectual awakening of mediæval Christianity.   The Christians had rejected the
seductive culture of later Rome, a sacrifice made in
the interests of religion.   And at first this seemed to
involve the ruin of intellectuality, by shutting off the
sources of pagan intellectual life.   But a harvest a
hundredfold greater than could have been obtained
from the worn out pastures of pagan intellect, was
reaped in the splendid intellectual outburst with which
the names of St. Thomas Aquinas, our own Scotus, and
the other great mediæval thinkers are associated.   So
the Irish movement, though shutting off certain poor
and polluted sources of English intellectuality, has
opened up a fresh and ever-broadening stream of
true native culture in our midst.

———◆———

XII.—Gaelicophile Poetry and Two New Poets.

NEWS from Helicon and Tir-na-nog!   Two
new poets!   Perhaps the collocation of the
two places just mentioned is not quite con-
gruous, but we are dealing with Anglo-Irish poetry,
and claim its franchises.   Provided there be a spice
of Greek and a leaven of Gaelic one should not
inquire further.   The poets in question are Mr.
MacDonagh, the author of *Through the Ivory Gate*,
and Mr. Gerald Griffin, whose *Lays of the Moy* lie
before me.   Both writers are Irishmen ; the works
of both are published in Dublin, and in one case, at
any rate, printed on Irish paper.   All these facts
make one feel more kindly towards these authors,
and notwithstanding the prejudice against Anglo-
Irish poetry which is running very strong at the
present moment, there is much of interest to be found
in their works.

I treat them together because there is a very large
element common to both.   They are members of a
new and rather interesting, if somewhat amusing,

school, which is a result of the Gaelic movement, even though its members write in English. They are in a transitional state. They write in English but want to write in Irish. They are eminently apologetic. They recognise the disfavour into which their partly English art has come—"One of these lazy poets ought to find time to learn Irish even if other people can't," is the ordinary man's reflection— and they seek to soothe us by holding out hopes of Irish lyrics in the future. Mr. MacDonagh* commits himself to promises, Mr. Griffin confines himself to the more subtle suggestiveness of Gaelic words and expressions inserted at intervals in his verse.

The school might well be called the Gaelicophile School of Poetry ; the word is, no doubt, a strange compound, but so is the school. We think it is largely founded on the really excellent book of poems of William Dara. In this work, which attained a well-merited success, owing to a Catholicity and spirituality that expressed themselves through the medium of a fresh native imagery, Mr. Byrne expressed a longing as evidently sincere as everything else in his little book to find voice for his imaginings in the Gaelic tongue, and I fear he has unintentionally set a fashion. He has given the elegiac poet a new unfulfilled desire, the lyrical misanthrope a new cause of complaint. The opportunity was too good to be lost by the woeful brethren, and I see that we shall have a race of bards mourning over their inability to speak Irish for the next half-century at any rate.

Now if this desire be sincere there is no objection to it. A man in O'Growney I. may yet be a poet. He may thirst to communicate his love to the muses. If the object of his passion were named Norah and were customarily in the habit of frequenting a well, or if she were the possessor of a spinning-wheel in a barn, and he sought to acquaint us with these facts,

---

* Since this was written Mr. MacDonagh has, I learn, become a very expert ʒᴀᴇʋᴇᴀⱡ.

no doubt he could and would essay to convey himself in his mother tongue. But his sentiments being
of a more intricate and less easily describable character, is he not justified in expressing himself as best
he may whilst he none the less utilises at suitable
intervals all the Gaelic at his command ? I am far
from throwing doubt on the Gaelic accomplishments
of either of the present writers, but to prevent a bad
custom creeping in, I suggest that future Anglo-
Irish poets should be compelled to append to each
lyric, as a guarantee of good faith, a certificate stat-
ing what part of O'Growney they have arrived at,
e.g., " A Sonnet to Leonora" (guttural aspiration),
" The Rejected Lover's Complaint" (eclipsis). We
should thus be enabled to gauge accurately the
fervour of the lyrist's enthusiasm for the Gaelic
language, admiring his verses the while.

Another peculiarity of both poets is a strong tendency to classical allusions, which are indeed common
enough in old Gaelic poems. In Mr. Griffin's book,
for example, the second stanza of one of his poems
begins:—

> " Diana's step on Ida's crest
>   Shows virgin liberty.
> And Venus, on Olympus' breast
>   Is airy, light, and free."

Perhaps it is due to British associations, but one
can't help feeling a slight shock when, on looking to
the top of the page, one sees that the air to which
this dithyramb is to be sung is " Irish Molly, Oh !"
Again, we meet with the lines :—

> " Oh ! Cupid, you're a blackguard, rare,
>   To torture thus my heart,
> But now, *ma bouchal*, just take care,
>   Or I will make you smart."

Would it be unkind to pick holes in the Gaelic of
" ma bouchal"?

In both writers there is a genuine love of their country and a strong spirit of Catholic piety. In Mr. MacDonagh this tone is the more remarkable, as his poems are seemingly intended to depict a conversion. The earlier ones display a state of doubt and painful indecision ; but peace is at length found in the consolations of religion. The second part of his collection is wholly devoted to Ireland. The bringing back of Roisin—who symbolises the spirit of Irish nationality—from Tir-na-nog, whither she had departed, is very beautifully described. And, though, in more than one instance one seems to detect an echo of William Dara, there is singular smoothness and delicacy in his verse. One feels always that if he is not a great creator of ideals, yet he has lived with the ideal. There ever clings to his lines the the fragrance of beauty.

His poems dealing with Ireland end in strange fashion. The whole burden of his song is one of revival, hope, and happiness. But his work is entitled *Through the Ivory Gate*, the Grecian symbol of false dreams. His last poem is entitled " Through the Horn Gate," the symbol of true dreams, and is a striking piece of compressed pessimism. It is the little red mouse that comes forth at the end. His dream of beauty ended, he would have it that he is thrown back on the terrible reality of Irish life. But this article is not the place to discuss whether he is right or wrong, for I must now take leave of our authors. I trust I have not angered the wild-eyed race of poets.

XIII.—Nationality and Amusements.

" HOW much better if this money were applied to some reproductive purpose." This is a phrase, which, sometimes rightly, sometimes wrongly used, is pretty familiar to Irishmen at the present time. Now and then we hear it used

of the money spent on drink, but more commonly
it rings in our ears as the catch-cry of the followers
of Moore and MacCarthy. Yet, in reality, it is
meaningless. It provides no alternative solution
whatsoever to the problem of how the money should
be spent, for if money is invested in some reproductive undertaking, the question of its proper use is
merely postponed. Unless it is to accumulate in-
definitely at compound interest and so be rendered
entirely useless, the question of its proper employment must some day come up for settlement.
Some, of course, will hoard all their earnings, but
most of us have not so great a regard for our heirs.
Might not, then, reformers, and especially temperance
reformers, consider more carefully how the money,
over and above necessary expenses, which is now
wasted, and which it is proposed to save, should for
the future be employed?

But, most people will say that the difficulty
which they find in life is not how to spend money,
but how to get it to spend. They are even inclined
to conjecture as a matter of speculation that, were
their incomes considerably increased, they would still
be equal to the task of disposing of them. It may
then seem somewhat of a paradox to maintain that
one of the chief obstacles to Irish progress is that Irish
people do not know how to spend money, and that,
if they did know how, they might, in the long run,
find it easier to earn it. I should feel considerable
hesitation in putting forward this doctrine, which
appears at first blush to controvert experience, were
the idea entirely my own. But it is not. Some
time since a gentleman, who was a recognised
authority on Irish economic problems,* observed
to me that one of the most important problems
for him who should seek to regenerate Ireland
economically was to create new wants and new
desires. Thus only by providing new inducements
for increased toil and greater enterprise could the

* The late Mr. W. Coyne, my beloved master.

country be raised out of the economic slough into which it has fallen, and that industrial spirit which is, perhaps, our most pressing need at the present moment, be brought into being.

The expenditure of the ordinary Irishman may at present be divided into three parts:—Expenditure on religion; secondly, the necessary and reasonable expenses of his position in life, house rent, necessary food, clothing, etc.; and lastly, drink, sport, and possibly some extravagance in dress and other externals, or even in food. They correspond with:— His spiritual duties; the duties of his position, and what he owes to his family; pleasures. Religious expenditure is, M'Carthy notwithstanding, an inconsiderable sum, whilst it is really one of the best uses to which money is put in the country. The second head is with the largest part of humanity, who have no very strong desire and very little opportunity of rising above their present social stratum a fixed charge. The item of pleasures, the variable quantity in the equation, is really the barometer of industrial effort. It increases with success; if a man relax his efforts, it is here that, unless he is prepared to incur absolute ruin, he will first begin to experience the pinch of failure. And in so far as a man looks to any material reward for his efforts, and how many are there whose nature is of so high a type that their sense of duty admits of no worldly alloy, in so far as a man casts any side glance at the temporal effects of strenuous effort, it is to the worldly pleasure which money represents that he must look as the material result of all his strivings. As, then, worldly pleasure is the human measure of successful effort, it is of no small moment to see that the pleasure is of the right sort.

What, then, does pleasure mean in Ireland? Into what do we in this country convert the money that we earn. One is not, then, far wrong in setting down the pleasures of the average man in Ireland as drink,

sport and extravagance. For with a vast number of our
people there is absolutely no other alternative. So
much is this the case that a clergyman, who is a
prominent temperance advocate, quite recently told
me that it has been remarked that where the Anti-
Treating League has succeeded and drinking been
lessened, betting has correspondingly increased. This
tends to show that when money is turned away from
flowing in an improper channel, there is at present no
proper channel in which it can run. Of course, there
are many cases where the money spent on drink has
been diverted from necessary household purposes, and
here temperance is an immense blessing. But I am
only referring to those who can afford what they
spend. In such cases, when drink is stopped, the only
alternative is sport. Not that sport is to be con-
demned. And those sports which are most healthful,
such as hurling, football, cycling, or swimming, are
commonly the least expensive. To be wholly absorbed in it, however, a condition common enough in
this country, is surely a state little to be desired. It
is the absolute exaltation of the animal side of our
being. Whilst, if that sport be a false one, one that
involves no exertion, such as racing or coursing, or
the gladiatorial pastime of professional football, lately
imported from England, absorption in it becomes a
devotion to pleasure of the lowest and least intellectual kind.

The spread of a desire for intellectual pleasures is,
in truth, one of the greatest needs of our country
to-day. At present our condition in this matter as a
nation is absolutely disgraceful. Not to speak of Art
or Music our neglect of all forms of literature is a bye-
word. If a Royal University Fellow or one of the
professors of Maynooth were to produce a work on
literature or philosophy to-morrow, it would probably, in most cases, have a sale of about twenty
copies in his own country. It is small wonder then
that you would be able to compile but a very defec-
tive list of Irish Catholic professors from the cata-

logue of the National Library. My readers may say, however, that, in all sincerity, they have not the money for such things. Perhaps, if they really desired them ardently, and if there were a fashion of buying them, they might somehow manage to find it. How few are prevented by poverty from buying theatre-tickets, for instance? Yet, grant that many suffer from inability, it is to the rich that we should look for support. But unfortunately rich Irishmen, and especially rich Catholics, are the worst offenders. To be able to hunt, or to keep a carriage, or a motor-car, is the be-all and end-all of their desires. And, if this be impossible, they find a consolation in frequent race-meetings. A work of literature they never think of buying, and even the sixpenny magazines and four-and-sixpenny novels, which form their chief mental pabulum, are imported from England. There are a large number of wealthy people in Ireland whose intellectual condition is precisely on a par with that of their coachmen.

This absence of intellectual interest is partly the result of past repression and misfortune, partly of present Anglicisation, that most deadly of mental opiates, and partly also of the absence of facilities for higher education. The work of the Irish movement, which makes intellectuality popular by making it national, is the most encouraging feature in the gloomy prospect. The Gaelic League has taught men to think; to seek other pleasures than those of animals; and it asks them to do this in the cause of Ireland. And from its efforts we may hope to see a revival of intellectual interest in Ireland, a revival that shall not oust true sport, but shall prevent complete absorption in those spurious forms which exercise neither mind nor body. There are a great number of persons, of course, whom you can never arouse to interest in intellectual matters; but there are a still greater number whom you can. With such an increase of intellectual desires must come an increased energy which shall seek to obtain

the means of gratifying them. From this energy
will spring increased prosperity; and, after virtue
prosperity and intellectuality are the chief glories of
manhood and nationhood alike.

——◆——

XIV.—The Philosophy of an Irish Theatre.

THE creation of a native theatre is perhaps the
most interesting task to which Irishmen can devote themselves. We are not a reading people.
But most Irishmen have a natural liking for the theatre,
and religious prejudices do not constitute an obstacle
with us as with the English. So we may reasonably hope that a really national drama could be
developed in our midst and made a vehicle of intellectual expression for ourselves, much as it is for so
many peoples on the continent. The drama is,
also, a form of composition specially suited for
bringing before our people productions in the Irish
tongue.

It is then a matter of some importance that our
new dramatic movement should be guided along
right lines, and I am inclined to share in the very
general fear that the aspirations of some members
of the National Theatre Society are not altogether
in the right direction. I have before me a statement
of Mr. Yeats as to his views on the purpose of
dramatic art. Roughly speaking they seem to be,
first, that a dramatist, if he writes merely as a
dramatist, "should have no propaganda but that of
Art," and secondly, that he should not be confined to
the accepted views of morality, but should be free to
see "with strange eyes," that is apparently to form a
new morality for himself. The first of these proposi-
tions is in substance no more than Aristotle taught
two thousand years ago; but from the latter view
as to a new morality, I very definitely dissent.

As for the first question, namely, the immediate
purpose of the drama; a play, like other works

of Art, may be composed with various objects in view : simply to amuse and so give pleasure, in which case the functions of the dramatist and the toffee-manufacturer appear to be much akin; or again, to give moral instruction (most plays of a propagandist nature fall under this heading); or yet to be a mental exercise and intellectual recreation; or, lastly, to elevate the soul by raising it to the contemplation of beauty. Plays which are composed with this last object are, alone, true Art, and I agree with Mr. Yeats that elevation, or, at least, elevation added to mental exercise, is the true purpose of drama. It is not therefore, the function of a play to impart moral instruction except incidentally; and it follows, of course, that the author should not set before him any particular propagandist purpose. The representation of the beautiful should be his true aim.

To hold that the true purpose of dramatic art is not moral instruction is, however, one thing, to allow the author that degree of moral freedom which Mr. Yeats would seem to claim for him is quite another. No doubt, in regard to a great many matters the author's moral views are not of any grave importance. A play advocating petty larceny or housebreaking could scarcely do serious harm, and even if it did the question might safely be left in the hands of the police. But in regard to certain subject-matters, and especially sexual morality and our attitude towards religion, the author has it in his power to do grave evil ; for his teaching will be followed, and being followed must produce its natural results. It is on such subjects that the critic has a right to make his voice heard, and that the Irish people have a right to protest if they find their *National* theatre tending towards immoral, anti-Christian or anti-human propaganda.

It is not merely the views on morality, which the author expresses, however, that may render a play objectionable. The moral of the last act in an English

D

drama is usually sound. It is the general tone of a play, the view of life conveyed by it, the selection of the morbid particular in preference to the healthy universal that makes a work repugnant to the moral sense. A dramatist may sometimes find it necessary to introduce, and in many circumstances is justified in introducing, elements in themselves objectionable; it is different when, as in much of contemporary French literature, the author's mind is evidently filled with such matters, and dwells with a morose satisfaction on the diseases of life. Such an attitude of mind was in great measure exhibited in *In the Shadow of the Glen*, and it was this rather than any moral it taught that made one turn away from it. And the *Playboy of the Western World* merely showed the same tendencies in a more aggravated form.

In treating of Art (of which dramatic Art is a species), I give that word a somewhat narrow definition. I confine the term to that form of imitation, be it through the medium of painting, sculpture, music or drama, which deals with the ideal, which endeavours, however imperfectly, to express the ideas in the mind of God, by representing something better than anything actually existing in the imperfect life which we see around us. Plays which deal with such subjects, and I conceive both Mr. Yeats's and Mr. Martyn's plays to do so, I call dramatic Art. And such plays alone are worthy of the honour which is paid to Art by all civilized communities. It is true that the term Art is frequently used in a different sense. It is applied to all forms of imitation, even including the farcical comedy or musical farce, or, at least, to such forms as convey instruction and supply a mental exercise by the original view of life and the clever representation of its circumstances which they present. The best comedies, such, for instance, as those of Molière, or the Anglo-Irish comedy-writers, belong to this class.

Yet though it may seem strange to say so, such plays are not Art, in the true sense of the

word. As being a vehicle of mental instruction
—not moral instruction—however, and an exciting
cause of thought they fulfil a useful function, a
much higher one than the musical farce. Their
object is, no doubt, amusement; and they are not
directed towards the high and lofty aim of true
Art. But the amusement is of an intellectual type;
and thus mental exercise and instruction result
from it. As such they impart a higher form of
pleasure than that derived from the mere drama of
enjoyment. And our object in Ireland, if we desire to
resist the debasing tendencies of Anglicisation should
be to make our pleasure of as high a type as possible,
that is, of as high a type as is consistent with real
enjoyment.

XV.—Silly People and the Irish Movement.

NO charge is more commonly levelled against
the Irish Movement by those who are half
converted to it, than the accusation that it
is of too puritan a character. Gaelic Leaguers maintain, it is objected, an undue standard of solemnity,
and everything from their newspapers to their concerts suffers from this failing. The charge is, in
truth, not altogether without foundation. You go to
a ᵇᵍoᵖᵘᵢᵈeᵃᵗᵗ with very different feelings from those
with which you visit some English form of amusement, say, some light piece at the theatre. At the
best enthusiasm takes the place of jollility, and your
sentiments are likely to be those of mental appreciation rather than mere enjoyment. Hence it comes
that not a few people are repelled from the Gaelic
League, because they consider it an enemy of mirth.

The argument of such critics whenever they
formulate it, might be reduced to this. You desire
an Ireland which shall be completely Gaelic, which
shall be as Gaelic as England is English, you hope

that your Gaelic League shall eventually embrace
every member of the population, why then do you
set yourselves to exclude elements which exist in
every other complete people in the world? Why
should you shut out the "Johnny," the sot and the
admirer of the low music-hall song from your Irish
Ireland? Are you quite sure that the sons of chief-
tains in the Gaelic period had a very elevated taste
in their popular ballads? Are there not things
in early Irish literature—as in all ancient literature—
that, if they were published to-day, your Irish-Irelander
would strongly condemn. In seeking to recreate
your nation, why should you set up an impossible
standard of excellence, such as no nation ever has
maintained or ever can maintain. Moderately stated
one might be ready to give some countenance to
these objections, but if pressed to their logical conclusion there is no one that would not revolt against
them. For carried to their furthest extreme they
imply that the Irish movement should encourage that
which is in itself immoral.

Such arguments leave out of consideration the fact
that the present Irish movement is essentially a propagandist one. In the fullness of time it may include
the whole country, bad men as well as good. But at
present it must seek as it has up to this done, to use
the best men in the community as its instruments.
Nothing has been more remarkable hitherto than the
moral effect of the Gaelic League. And this has won it
many friends who are perhaps but little convinced
by the case for the movement on its merits. Even
its opponents have had to bear testimony to the
excellent work it is doing from a moral and social
standpoint. The bitterest enemy of the League can
scarcely deny that its members are some of the most
upright, sober and honest men in the community. If
you know that a young fellow is in the Gaelic
League, by that very fact you know a number of
other favourable things about him as well. And
such a reputation must be of enormous assistance to

THE IDEA OF A NATION.

its propaganda. No doubt this good repute arises in large part from the fact that it is the best types in the community who join the Gaelic League. Yet to some extent it springs from the intrinsic nature of the movement; for it is essentially a movement of self-denial; the man who gives up his ease to learn a difficult language for his conntry's sake is practising something very much akin to religious mortification, and reaps, in the result, the abundant fruits of his acts.

Moral elevation is, then, one of the strongest recommendations of the Irish movement, and it is the part of its activity that the League can least afford to abandon. It must ever remain the enemy of bad plays, corrupt papers and low songs. It is the sterling character of the men who belong to it, and especially of the early Gaelic Leaguers that has made it the success that it is. And few will venture to claim that it should be morally degraded. But what of intellectual elevation? As the Irish movement has stood for moral improvement, so it has also stood for an intellectual awakening. Under its influence the country is beginning to think. In Art, Music and Literature, save where the limitations of Irish existence have stood in its way, it has always sought to encourage a far higher intellectual standard than that to be found in the life of contemporary England or Anglo-Ireland. And hence it is that plays for instance, inspired by the Irish movement sometimes fall under censure as being above the average man. For as the Irish movement is the friend of morality, so it is the sworn enemy of silliness and vulgarity. And it is as much opposed to an empty as to a vicious mind.

As to the moral question there cannot then be any doubt; as to the intellectual policy, however, there may well be hesitation especially on the grounds referred to at the beginning of the article. We wish to make our movement as wide-spread as possible. We may, however, reasonably exclude vicious men; are we

equally justified in excluding silly men? Nay more,
for the sake of maintaining a high intellectual
standard, a fine thing in itself, are we justified in
alienating that large class, who are not now intellectual and who are most clearly determined that they
never shall be. They will do as good a day's work
or punt a football as far as any man. And your silly
man is often a useful and true-hearted member of the
community; so is your confirmed unintellectual. Both
may have sound national sentiments. Should we
then have silly songs, silly jokes and silly plays—all
of an Irish flavour—to encourage him? All wise
politicians cater for the silly man; should the Gaelic
League also make provision for him? Quite recently
I remember hearing a song about a parrot sung at a
concert; it was quite harmless and perfectly absurd,
yet I am sure it would have been hissed at a ᵳᵵᴑᴘᴜᴉ-
ᴠᴇᴀᴄᴛ. But such a ditty is what your silly man
delights in. Should we then seek to attract him
by having Gaelic absurdities about parrots?

I am afraid that the problem itself may seem somewhat
silly. Yet, there is really something in the question;
as to how far should the Irish movement seek to make
elevation and intellectuality a condition of its activity?
This has in the main been its policy up to the present, and the result is both loss and gain. The
intellectuality is certainly a gain; but none the
less an extensive and highly respectable class of the
community is somewhat arbitrarily excluded. And I
suppose the true solution must be something in the
nature of a compromise. "Silliness in moderation"
should be the motto of reformers. Healthy amusement of a lighter sort, for which even the most intellectual man is at times disposed, is certainly badly
wanted. And comic songs and comedies, which shall
not be vulgar or anti-Irish are a crying need in
Ireland just at present. For the English comic song
with which we are familiar, even if unobjectionable in
other respects, is by no means funny, and is, as a rule,
wholly out of harmony with Irish ideas of humour.

It is little more than fashion that makes Irishmen laugh
at it. And a few good Irish comic songs would have a
success entirely on their merits. I venture to think,
if it be not treason to say so, that the Gaelic League
might like the poet condescend to *desipere in loco,*
and whilst remaining intellectual, might yet on occasion relapse into frivolity without detriment.

XVI.—A Tea-Shop Idyil.

LOVE-MAKING is proverbially expensive for
the male participant in the transaction. Even
an afternoon devoted to adoration on one side
and the consumption of chocolate creams (let us
hope of Irish confection) on the other, results in a
financial deficit to the admirer. The more reason
that I should inform my readers of a new process
which I have discovered all by accident; it is no
less than a method by which the cost of that most
pleasing pastime may be reduced to a minimum—in
fact to the humble sum of fourpence. Need I say
that the process is of West British invention. My
discovery was the result of chance. Passing the
doors of the —— Restuarant, with a West British
acquaintance, one evening, I began to feel that it
was tea-time. "Come in and have coffee," quoth I.
He replied by enquiring who was the object of my
affections. Somewhat astonished, I hastened to
explain that hunger, and not love, was the feeling
uppermost in my bosom at the moment. "Why,
d —— it, you don't mean to say that! Oh! I forgot
that you were one of the Cıonnuıʃ ʧá ʧú's," he replied,
and when we went in I began to understand. We
had rashly entered the holy of holies—this was the
home of the sixpenny Johnny, the temple of his
fourpenny flirtations. We were surrounded by him.
The sixpenny bank clerk strove to outshine the
sixpenny sizar from Trinity, but both were done out

by the youthful *militaire*. Fresh from the glories of
the militia he swaggered in twos and threes round
the fire-place, and his resplendent fancy waistcoat
was as a nipping frost to the hopes of the "men"
from "college," his would-be rivals. "Beastly Boah!
the doocid old War Office won't let us chaps out to
the fwont. I say, Biddy, w'ere's the band?" So
said the hero. The faculties of the lady addressed
seemed suddenly to spring into animation. Quitting
the medico, who was playfully projecting lumps of
sugar at her, and leaving the lady who was wildly
gesticulating for boiled milk, and the old gentleman
who ever and anon expressed a mournful longing for
scones, to pursue their fruitless task, she hastened to
pay court to the waistcoat. The medico looked hurt,
his two companions began to quiz him; he was fain
to bury himself in a sugar cake, but he soon found
consolation in some humorous and sprightly pas-
sages with the girl who brought him his bill.

Meantime we waited patiently, contemplating a
platter of fancy bread. Beautiful creatures passed us
and repassed us, but coffee remained a distant hope;
we did not seem to be of the favoured few. We
thought of appealing to the lady in black, but she
seemed quite as occupied as her subordinates, differ-
ing from them mainly in the fact that her circle of
admirers was more *elite*. At last the waistcoat left
for Grafton Street. The boiled milk lady was
furiously ringing a broken bell. The old gentleman
was beginning to hiss. The fair attendant advanced
our way. My companion winked and said : "Hello,
Biddy! that's a pretty flour." "Go on," giggled
the female humorist, "I don't mind you." The
manœuvre was successful; we got our coffee, and
cut out even the old business man who was smirking
in the distance. "I told you so," said my companion, "you're not minded here unless you're
amatory."

Such is a Dublin tea-room. Unlimited amatori-
ness for fourpence ! What a prospect for the *hell-of-a*

fellow! The various tea-rooms that have sprung up in our midst have undoubtedly helped on the temperance cause, so far as young fellows of the middle class are concerned. But they have had one curious result; they have produced the tea-drinking "hell-of-a-fellow," the coffee and scones rake. No doubt he is better than his bar-frequenting brother. His antics are harmless, but he is very funny. His joy is to bring in some novice (the joint banquet won't exceed a shilling) and show what a villain he is, and how he can flirt. On the whole we ought to be glad that "villainy" should assume so harmless a form. If they weren't West British we should have left them in peace. Five* years hence the youthful "rakes' " may laugh at themselves, whilst if the uninitiated find it upon occasions somewhat difficult to obtain food in these establishments, they can at least get entertainment during the interval of waiting by looking on at the pranks of our youthful West Britons.

XVII.—Respectability and Nationality. ¶

RESPECTABILITY is essentially a comparative term, denoting a thing that has little reality behind it; yet it exercises a very real and powerful influence on the actions and thoughts of mankind. To be "respectable" really means little more than to be what you are at any given moment as compared with somebody else—to be the engine-driver as compared with the stoker, the stoker as compared with the boy that cleans the boiler. Yet "to be respectable" is the sole aim and object of a vast deal of human endeavour; and with women especially the motive is all-powerful. It is not for itself, however, that I would now consider respectability, but merely for the purpose of dealing with its effect on

* It is five years since the article was written.

the movement for nationality, a question of no little importance.

The Language movement and the Irish Language itself have found one of their most deadly foes in this eagerness for respectability. The injury caused by it is nowadays not as serious as it was a few years since, yet it is still very considerable. When the Irish speaker abandons his native tongue for English, he has generally only one motive, respectability; he hopes to be thought better than his neighbour who still uses his mother tongue. So until recently the movement to revive the Irish Language was not thought respectable by the middle classes as a whole. And the upper middle classes still abhor things Irish for a like reason. Now when a movement is not deemed respectable, it calls for no little courage in a man to join it; but, in the present condition of society, it requires almost super-human self-denial on the part of a woman to enable her to prove superior to the prejudices of her set. And one finds as a result that in the case of women as in the case of men to a lesser degree, the movement for Nationality stops short at a certain definite social stratum, and the region of Irish dancing and Gaelic song does not reach beyond it. Of course, there are broad-minded exceptions in all classes, but as a whole the statement is substantially true. It is to be observed, however, that the movement, which has already won the support of the masses, is gradually extending its sway and moving upwards, as the classes slowly but gradually fall one by one beneath its influence. And many a man is now an ardent supporter of the Gaelic League, who thought it several classes beneath him a few years ago.

Respectability then, it will be seen, acts as a re-tardative force on the movement for Nationality, by making each class, when the Irish movement is pre-sented to it, turn away from it, as being a charac-teristic possession of the class immediately beneath it in the social scale. And this is particularly true of the other sex, which is naturally conservative and fearful of innovations that are "not the thing." Of course, in the long run the class that refuses will also be conquered, and the same process will be repeated with the class immediately above. But meantime the process of persuasion is a slow one, and a great number of the best educated and wealthiest members of the community keep away from the movement. The crave for respectability and its treatment is then, by no means a useless study for those who have the Language movement at heart.

This, however, is not the only result of "respectability." It is also responsible for a peculiar reaction, which is the converse of the tendency I have alluded to. The proposition advanced by high-class recusants (of course, throughout I only use such terms as "high" in their accepted conventional sense) that to be National is to be wanting in respectability, easily leads to the opinion that to be respectable is to be wanting in Nationality. This logical deduction from a falsehood is, perhaps, commoner in Ireland than at first sight appears. There is a strong tendency to suspect the motives and the Nationality of one who is much "higher" in social position than yourself. There is always a strong inclination to suspect something wrong about a very well-dressed Irish-Irelander, even though "well-dressed" is again eminently a comparative term. And the result is, of course, to strengthen the false converse statement that Nationality is not respectable, and to make the capture of the higher classes slower and more difficult. "Better without them," perhaps, some one will say—a remark which will show that he, too, has been captured by the theory that Nationality and respectability are inconsistent.

No doubt if such a doctrine were carried to its logical conclusion it is capable of a *reductio ad absurdum*. For respectability being merely comparative, every class except the very lowest, that is, possibly, except the criminal class, would in turn be excluded. In Ireland, however, the anti-respectable idea has a more solid basis of fact than the false democracy of inter-class prejudice, which causes shop-keepers to denounce the aristocracy in England and the labouring classes to denounce shop-keepers in France and Germany. For Ireland is not a homogeneous country; it is in an unnatural condition. The top has been knocked off society in our land, and a foreign top imported from England and imperfectly soldered on. Our native aristocracy, for what it was worth, is gone. We have instead an imported substitution, which has not as yet fused with our population, and has ever been a source of irritation in the body politic. When the greater number of those who compose the upper or more "respectable" classes are un-Irish or anti-Irish, it is easy to understand how it comes about that the higher any man's social position, the more his motives are viewed with suspicion, a suspicion that in the circumstances must often be well-founded.

Our object should, however, be to embrace all classes; not that we should waste our energy in preaching to unconvertible Ulster immigrants. We should seek, however, to recreate a national aristocracy and a national professional class. For we have need of wealthy men and intellectual men. Witness the good done by such men who *have* joined us. And we should be slow to thrust aside wealth or education as connoting anti-nationality. We should rather be ready to bear with the foibles inseparable from wealth in weak human nature; and if his heart be sound we should suffer our plutocrat to over-dress himself or think himself "class" to his heart's content. The fault of the "all creeds and classes" dogma has generally been that it sought to treat as a part of the Irish nation those who did not belong to it, or desire to be belong to it, at all. But with regard to those who are really of it, or wish to be of it, the people of Ireland should not mean any section of the people, however large, but the Irish nation as a whole.

XVIII.—Of Sourness.

(With Apologies to Bacon.)

" *Tristis illi vultus*," saith Seneca of Cato the Censor
the which were likewise true of many in our own
time. There be them that have a sourness of visage
as it were a part of their natures. The which hath
been thought to be a sign of salvation, as they being
like to have sure warrant of the life to come, whom
this doth please so ill; and in truth they had need
of compensation for their ill-favouredness. Yet stern-
ness of countenance is not all times insignal of virtue
as there be herbs that being bitter are yet unwhole-
some. Indulgence being but possible on fit occasion,
and as it were *per saltum*, a man hath won't to be
grave in the intermission of his pleasures. Such a
one is oftentimes deemed pious by them that see
only his regrets. So, too, there be that by seeming
sad would gain the repute of sanctity, as practising
self-denial. The which in truth is a reputation
more sought for by churchmen than those of Rome,
whose piety hath less of satisfaction and more of
fearfulness. The piety of judges hath oft been noted
and hath in truth ever something of sterness; but
advocates and counsel have little of it, as being much
in affairs and having yet something to long for, before
salvation. Sourness sits ill on a woman, for she shall
be thought pious without it; yet you shall oftentimes
see it in spinsters, who feign a contempt for them
that be married. Sectaries are won't to be sour, for
thus they shall outdistance them that conform. So,
too, such as dwell in suburbs, for being closer con-
gregated, their sadness doth more react, the one on
the other, and there is greater strife of justification.
As they of Rome have days of fast so there be many
that fast from mirth of a Sunday, as among the

Scots, where it is related you shall e'en whistle at peril. So you shall see many a one sour on the Sabbath, that hath little heed of godliness in his daily employ. They that be vicious in youth are wont to be sour in age. There is a sourness of railways; so, too, bone-dealers, bankers, and professors. The middle class hath commonly more of severity than the nobles being minded to excel in sanctity if not in dignity. Sourness hath oftentimes a coat of sugar, whereby it is more easily received, yet you shall taste it anon like aloes in a pill. Of a truth, sourness hath wont to be the quality of wines of the baser sort, so too of men.

XIX.—The Island of Protestants.

IN politics there is often much to be gained by concealing the truth from others; there is seldom any advantage in concealing it from yourself. Were it possible by any machination to persuade the people of England that Mr. Sloan and Mr. William Moore were Catholics, or that the Plantation counties had now been entirely engulfed by the waters of the Bann, I should be ready to join a conspiracy directed to effecting that nefarious purpose. But I have never been able to see what is to be gained by deluding *ourselves* into this geographical heresy. Various people may suggest different modes of dealing with your Ulster anti-Irishman—your Southern and Western alien, already half-absorbed, won't count in the long run—but what on earth is the good of pretending to completely ignore his existence. For you can no more talk Protestant Ulster into Irishry than Ireland can be argued into Englishry, and in the days of the newspaper and the telegraph it is impossible to entirely conceal the existence of three quarters of a million persons.

"We are an island of Protestants, surrounded on

three sides by Roman Catholics, and on the fourth by the ocean," was the apt description of the circumstances given by a deceased divine. He desired to indicate, presumably, that the islanders had about as much connection with the Irish on the one flank as with the mermen and mermaids on the other. And anyone who looks into the matter will find that his geography was substantially correct, that roughly speaking the Protestants of Ulster form a solid, contiguous mass of human beings—are, in fact, a denominational (or, if they prefer it, undenominational) island. They form a sort of anti-Ireland within our Ireland. And, it is not because of their religion that they do not form a part of the nation ; the reason of their not being Irish is, in truth, childishly simple— namely, that they do not happen to be Irishmen, and have no desire to become such.

How should we deal, then, with these poor islanders who cling obstinately to their corroborees and native habits now that we have discovered them? Let us first admit honestly that they *are* alien immigrants. There is no glossing over the fact. They are not Irish, and they don't want to be. They have never read a line of Davis in their lives, and they would grow sad if they thought they should be compelled to read him after their deaths. The best way to appreciate the position of these Ulsterians is to imagine them to be countrymen of their national hero, William. Now, if three quarters of a million Dutchmen or Transvaalers had their residence in the North-east of Ireland, should we consider them Irishmen ? and if they were, moreover, according to statistics, the most criminal, and the least moral inhabitants of Ireland, should we put ourselves out of our way to absorb them against their will ? Would it not be more reasonable to do as the Liberals have done in the Transvaal—grant them autonomy, and let them cultivate the civic virtues at their leisure ? Botha federated Africa and a federated Ireland may come later.

Now, this question is not a mere matter of theory, but rather one of great practical importance at the present moment. For the government of this island of Protestants is the one real difficulty in the way of either administrative or any other kind of Home Rule. As to the South and West of Ireland, the Land Act has deprived all the old lies about Protestant oppression, of the indispensible modicum of truth. The commission of any crime against a Protestant, as such, is altogether unknown, as testified at the recent General Assembly. Again, no less a person than Chamberlain pointed out with virulent truthfulness that the English have not much to fear from present-day Ireland, since, even during the Boer War, nothing was attempted against them. Remove the Ulster difficulty, and you have no longer any obstacle save carrion-crow mendacity to deal with.

Now, if we once face the problem of East Ulster honestly and courageously, if we cease to conceal from ourselves self-evident truths and difficulties it is possible to solve it. There will, of course, be those individual injustices and difficulties in detail that beset every measure of reform, but, on the whole, we shall be able to do substantial justice. The policy I advocate is Home Rule within Home Rule—that is, Home Rule for the alien wherever he exists in overwhelming numbers, which, for practical purposes, might be considered to be a three-fourths majority. Suppose the government of Ireland—or a large share of it—committed to a Lord Lieutenant bound like the King to act on the advice of an *elected*, and therefore *responsible*, minister, or suppose that government entrusted to a Council, as in the recent Bill. Now each county should have the option of refusing to come under this scheme. If it so refused it might be dealt with in either of two ways. Either it might have its affairs administered direct from London, a policy easy to adopt, and not unattractive to your Ulster West Briton, or else it might be permitted to, so to speak,

THE IDEA OF A NATION.

continue the old arrangement, and declare that, *as far as its affairs were concerned*, the English Lord Lieutenant should act not on the directions of the elected Irish minister or council, but exclusively on the advice of the English Cabinet or the English Chief Secretary, if there were one. Of course, *either* one or the other of these policies would have to be adopted. If it were the latter, a fair division of patronage and finance between the Irish minister or council and the English Chief Secretary, looking after Ulster interests, would have to be made.

It will be at once evident, however, that if existing county divisions were retained, the arrangement would work very harshly. A large minority might be unnecessarily expatriated or "impatriated" against its wishes. But several Northern counties are in numbers extremely large, and it might therefore be provided that wherever there was a district containing at least twenty thousand people, it might, upon petition (with the consent of three-fourths of the electors resident in it), have itself formed into a separate administrative county. On the other hand where a three-fourths majority of the inhabitants desired it, any district should be permitted to have itself added to a contiguous county. In this way the number of persons governed against their will in Ireland would be reduced to a minimum.

———◆———

XX.—The Partition of Ulster.

I SHALL now give the details of the scheme. The two principles to be adopted in any division of Ireland are first, that as many as possible of the Protestant immigrants should be left to govern themselves, or to be governed by Great Britain, according as they desired, with permission, of course, to throw in their lot with Ireland, if they so wished ; and secondly, that as few real Irish—which in Ulster practically means Catholics—as possible should be left under the sway of the stranger. My idea is

E

therefore, that (1) districts where Catholics are in a majority ; and (2) districts where, as in so many districts of the County Fermanagh, Catholics and Protestants live together in about equal proportion, should alike remain part of Ireland ; but that, as against this (3) districts where Protestants are in an overwhelming majority should, if they wished, be left free to shift for themselves. The machinery by which this result would be achieved would, however, be *local option* by counties and districts, as outlined in the last essay. The scheme would, therefore, be essentially *permissive*, giving free scope to Irish patriotism in Ulster, if any such were unexpectedly found to exist. Let us see how the scheme would work.

For the moment I put aside the cities of Belfast and Derry which involve a special problem. I should add that in my calculation I only use round numbers.

I first deal with the population outside the cities of Derry and Belfast, each side has to make some surrender. The result will be :—

Surrendered.

Ulster Protestants under Irish Rule.	Catholics under Protestant Rule.
200,000	95,000.

Enfranchised.

Free Ulster Protestants.	Free Ulster Catholics. (Under Irish Rule.)
500,000.	497,200.

Roughly speaking, we should have in Ulster, outside the cities—

$\frac{1}{2}$ million self-governing Protestants.

$\frac{1}{2}$ million self-governing Catholics.

$\frac{1}{4}$ million non-free of both.

By "non-free" I mean subjected to a system of government of which they disapprove. It will be seen that the number left in that condition is in my scheme very small, the number of Catholics so circumstanced being less than a hundred thousand.

Now, to come to details, four counties would be left entirely to Ireland. They are the Counties of Cavan, Monaghan, Donegal, and Fermanagh. The first three are overwhelmingly Catholic, and the population of the fourth is so mixed throughout that it could not well be locally separated. These proposals would involve leaving under Irish rule in these counties the following bodies of Protestants :—

	Non-free Protestants.	Non-free Catholics.
Cavan	16,500	0
Monaghan	20,000	0
Donegal	36,000	0
Fermanagh	29,000	0

A slight rectification of frontier between Donegal and the Protestant County of Londonderry might, however, possibly be carried out. There remain five counties to be dealt with—Tyrone, Londonderry, Armagh, Down, and Antrim. My proposals for these counties involve the following :—

	Non-free Protestants.	Non-free Catholics.
Tyrone	46,000	4,000
Londonderry	10,500	18,000
Armagh	17,000	14,600
Down	30,000	22,500
Antrim	1,100	36,000

TYRONE would substantially remain to Ireland, but would be subject to some edging off in the border parishes of Killyman, Aghaloo, Carnteel, part of Clonfeacle, part of Desertgreat, Derryloran, Artrea, Ballyclos and Tamlaght. These parishes would be added to Antrim or Armagh.

As to LONDONDERRY, it would be divided into two counties—(1) LONDONDERRY, in the North; and (2) DERRY, in the South. The parish of Tamlaght-ard would be added, if possible, to Donegal, Derry would consist roughly of the Catholic parishes of Killelagh, Dungiven, Banagher, Ballynascreen and Learmount, together with the equally mixed parishes of (with some division and edging off) Fauganvale, Lower Cumber, Upper Cumber, Maghera (part of), part of Ballyscullion, part of Desertmartin, part of Magherafelt, part of Artrea, part of Ballinderry. Derry would thus contain about 35,000, a very decent-sized county, and Londonderry about 70,000.

ARMAGH presents a comparatively simple problem, except for the town of Armagh itself. This town would fall into the same category with Belfast and Derry City, and should receive similar treatment. I leave it aside for the present. Armagh could be divided into two counties—(1) N. ARMAGH, containing about 70,000; (2) S. ARMAGH, containing about 50,000. The new county S. ARMAGH, containing about 33,000 Catholics and 17,000 Protestants, would be composed of the Catholic parishes of Killevy, Forkhill, Jonesboro', and Creggan, and of the mixed parishes of Newtownhamilton, Ballymyre, Lisnadill, Keady, Derrynoose, Tynan, English, Grange, and Clonfeacle (part of).

Down, likewise, is easily capable of division, containing a Catholic district in the South, a mixed district on the Eastern sea-board, and a Protestant district in the North and West. There would be two administrative counties—S. DOWN and N. DOWN. SOUTH DOWN would contain the Catholic parishes of Kilgoo, Kilkeel, Clonduff, Kilbroney, Clonallan and Newry, Rathmullen, Ballee, Dunsfort, and Ardglas, together with the following mixed parishes— part of Drumcath, part of Donaghmore, part of Annaclone, part of Drumgooland, Kilmega, Loughlinisland, Maghera, Down, Ballyculter, Ballyphilip, Ardquin, Ballytristan, Castleboy, and part of Ardkeel. This new county of SOUTH DOWN would contain about 42,000 Catholics and 30,000 Protestants. The town of Newry, though it is here included, is really in the same case with Belfast, Derry and Armagh, save that Catholics are in a large majority; its case is discussed below. Antrim is all Protestant, with the exception of "The Glens." Here Catholics are in a large majority (6,300 Catholics; 1,100 Protestants). This district might receive separate treatment as the outpost of Ireland. It could be added to the administrative county of SOUTH DOWN, or to Catholic Belfast.

This is the fairest division between Catholic and Protestant that could be made if division is to be attempted. Some people may think the half-and half districts comprised in the above ought to be differently treated in whole or in part, so as, for instance, to make a more equal division between subject Catholics and subject Protestants. I give their figures roughly. They are only in three counties:—

HALF-AND-HALF DISTRICTS.		PROTESTANT.	CATHOLIC.
Londonderry	... ...	12,000	14,000
Armagh	... ...	12,600	13,000
Down	... ...	16,700	12,800
Whole Borderland	...	41,300	39,800

It will be seen that the whole land debateable (outside Tyrone and Fermanagh) contains only 81,000 people. Round about the parish of Ardstraw, in the County Tyrone, there is a district where Protestants are in a majority, and similarly in the adjacent northern portion of Fermanagh, but from their position and from the mixed nature of the N. Fermanagh parishes, they could not very well receive separate treatment. For it should be pointed out clearly that, with the suggested exception of the Antrim Glens, a line can be drawn round the whole district proposed to be excluded; there is no breaking up into parcels.

Now as to the cities. Following our principles, Derry, Newry, and Armagh, being mixed, should fall to the share of Ireland, and Belfast, being overwhelmingly Protestant, to the other side. But this arrangement is not very satisfactory, so an attempt to give special treatment might be made in each case. There are about 35,000 Catholics living together between the Falls Road and the Railway in West Belfast. They are quite enough to form a city, an administrative county in themselves, amounting to almost three times the population of Kilkenny city, and twice that of county Longford. Whether any other districts could be also added, I do not know. The new city of *Devlinstown* would, no doubt, be a source of long-continued delight to the Orange population living

outside its boundaries. Similarly, owing to the tendency to live in quarters it might be possible to
divide Derry, Newry, and Armagh. The Protestant
quarters in Newry and Armagh would, of course, be
added to the Protestant County of *N. Armagh*. The
district round the Cathedral would fall to the Catholics
in Derry. A disadvantage in such an arrangement would
be that the poor quarters of a city, which are supposed
to be supported by the rich, would be separated from
them. This might, however, be got over, and in any
case the poor of Dublin have derived little benefit from
their statutory right to get a contribution from the
rich townships outside its boundaries.

The proposal is, therefore, simply this: The counties
of ANTRIM, DOWN, ARMAGH, and LONDONDERRY
would have the right to opt for Irish or for separate
government. If they chose separate government,
then, the counties of *S. Down*, *S. Armagh*, and
Derry would have a right to form themselves and
the parishes I have referred to in Tyrone to get
themselves added to Antrim or Armagh. So, too,
Catholic Belfast and Derry would have a right to
demand independence, and Protestant Newry and
Armagh to have themselves joined to N. Armagh.
The newly-formed counties would then again have a
right to chose for themselves. Outside the cities
(and apart from " The Glens"), the East Ulster Protestants would thus inhabit an unbroken portion of
Ireland by themselves.

————◆————

XXI.—Free Ulster and Federated Ireland.

IN proposing to divide a portion of Ulster from the
rest of the island, I know that I am running
counter to many sentimental considerations. I
am acting in direct contravention of the ideas of
Davis and all those who look upon every man born in
this island as an actual or potential Irishman. Were
such a statement made of those of alien race, who
dwell in the South and West of Ireland, I should be
inclined to agree with it. It is inconceivable that

were Ireland free the Protestants of the South could long hold out in opposition. In so far as they are kept apart from their fellow-countrymen, it is *class* hatred that keeps them so, and in a free and well-governed country class hatred is not an enduring force. It gives way before the first national crisis. Had Ireland got Home Rule in 1885, the Parnell Split would probably have seen the Southern Irish Protestant fighting side by side with the Irish Catholic on one side or the other.

With the North, however, the case is different. Here it is a matter of *race* distinction and *race* hatred. There is no good-humoured dallying with the Irish language in that part of the world; there are no devolutionists. Nothing could, in truth, really illustrate the difference between the Northern and Southern Protestant better than Lord Dunraven's movement and Mr. Sloan's. Lord Dunraven's is a movement of persons who are prevented by their class interest from giving full play to national sympathy. They love Ireland, but not the Irish party. Sloan's, on the contrary, is a movement of men who are hindered in giving full play to their democratic sympathies by their desire to preserve their racial freedom and integrity. And Michael Davitt would have been dear to them if he were not an Irishman. No doubt, the exceptional position of a subject community sometimes brings the two parties into an unnatural alliance, but in a free country the Sloanites and the devolutionists would be natural enemies.

It has always struck me that the attitude of Ireland towards the Ulsterman is not a little like that of the English towards ourselves. We both endeavour to gloss over the existence of the horrid thing, and hope without reason for a more united future. "We are all Britons; think of the Dublin Fusiliers," says the Englishman. "We are all Irish; think of '98," say we ourselves. And both parties refuse to admit any evidence to controvert the general proposition. Now, in reality the chances of our absorbing Ulster under Home Rule, and of England

absorbing us if we do not get it, are about equal.
It may be done, but it will take some doing, and
just men will prefer not to see that doing. "But
we do not mean to injure the Ulsterman; we shall
give him equal rights with ourselves," say we. And
the Englishman says the same of us. No doubt,
except in times of turmoil the Ulsterman would
enjoy complete outward personal freedom under
Home Rule. His property would not be liable to
confiscation, his house or his person to violence.
But *we* enjoy all these benefits as long as we do not
violate the law. We are not even liable to arbitrary
arrest upon mere suspicion like a Belgian or an
Austrian. And yet, say the English, you are not
happy. Nothing, not even liberty, contents you. Of
course, the point is that though we enjoy a very large
measure of *personal* freedom, though we may even
talk treason to our own and our fellow-countrymen's
hearts' content, we do not enjoy *political* freedom.
We are subject to a system of government which is
not *our* government—a system to which we object,
and with which we have no sympathy, which
involves the reward of the traitor and the degradation of the patriot, a system under which it is
impossible to disregard the fact that religion, unless
sterilised by complaisancy, is a ground of exclusion
from public office and emolument, a system under
which political shame and degradation have brought
about industrial stagnation and economic decay.

And this is precisely what the East Ulster
Unionists dread. They are not Irish, and they don't
want to become Irish, nor to suffer for not becoming so.
I do not believe it is really so much a desire for Irish
plunder that moves them. For the bulk of the Ulster
body, alike the Sloanite and the Presbyterian, get
but little of the plunder. It is the middlemen of
Unionism—the Dublin gang—that come in for most
of it. But it is the dread of race absorption, added to
that of religious domination, that really moves the
North, and makes them fervent in their opposition to
any scheme of Home Rule. That they are sincere in

this opposition it is mere futility to deny. If they had any desire to join us, with all their faults, we should be very glad to have them. But they have no such desire. And they have adopted precisely the same methods of propagating their opinions that we have ours. The press, the platform, and the ballot-box have all borne witness to their national faith, and it seems to me that if these persons demand their national independence, and if they are, in truth, distinct in nationality, it requires a strong reason to prevent their getting it. And, in my view, neither the fact of their dwelling on confiscated Irish soil, nor the fact that their freedom must involve the continuance in subjection of about a hundred thousand Irishmen, a number little greater than the subject Irish in Glasgow, is sufficient reason for such a denial. But, of course, if the choice has to be made, on the principle of choosing the lesser evil we should prefer a subject Ulster to the subject Ireland of our own times.

Again, even to those who seek a United Ireland it seems to me that, paradox though it be, the separation of East Ulster is the best way to attain that ideal if it be at all possible. We are wont to use the argument that Home Rule will mean a United Empire. For us the freedom of Ulster will, very possibly, bring about a similar result. In modern times a small minority is generally much better treated than a large one. The Catholics in Trinity College get on excellently because they are so few. And the Protestants in Ireland and the Catholics in Ulster would fare well, I believe, for this very reason. The Catholics in Ulster, for instance, would very probably have the favourable position of being the make-weight in the denominational scale between the Church of Ireland and the Presbyterians. There would be no longer any Catholic versus Protestant bitterness, and, after a time, as Irish industries developed, and the North and South become more economically one, it is not impossible that East Ulster might, of its own free will, become united to Ireland, just as the Transvaal will probably one day become, of its own free will, a

state in a United Africa, and as the several Australian states have already, of their free will, become
federated into an Australian Commonwealth.

————◆————

XXII.—Cosmopolitanism and Nationality.

NATIONALITY is, throughout the Western
world, the greatest living force of modern
times.   It saved Europe from Napoleonic
despotism.   It made Germany.   In our own day it is
saving smaller races from German and Russian oppression, and with the awakening of the Eastern races, it
must, in the future, have effects still more profound. It
is no small thing this, for which men are ready to
lay down their lives, this force to which the most
powerful governments have had to yield, this something in the minds of weak, helpless men that can
conquer armies and wear away strong tyrannies.

Yet at first sight nationhood may seem a bad thing,
this domestic squabble, this family pride that is forever
causing trouble in the household of humanity.   Why
should we maintain these barriers tangible or intan-
gible that shut off man from man ?   And why cherish
this distinction that sets men murdering one another?
Were not the broad spirit of humanity better, that
recognises no distinction between citizens of the
earth and gives no cause for racial bitterness.   In
Ireland such a question has not indeed much apposite-
ness.   For the alternatives set before us are not
whether we shall be national or cosmopolitan,
whether citizens of Ireland or citizens of the earth,
but whether we shall remain Irishmen or be absorbed
in the English nation, the people, who, of all others,
are most insular in the worst sense of the term, and
show least good-will and fellowship in their dealings
with foreign neighbours.   In fact whatever be the case
elsewhere we in Ireland can conscientiously comply
with both ideals at once, for as we cease to be Irish,
we must necessarily become more English, and therefore less cosmopolitan in any good sense of the word.

Is there really, however, so much opposition between the two ideals of universal brotherhood and
national unity? Is the smaller association in reality
the contradictory of the larger, and is it the experience of modern times that according as national
bonds have been strengthened the sense of brotherhood has been lost? If taking two countries where
national feeling is very strong we compare the relations of a Hungarian towards a Frenchman in our day
with those existing in feudal times, when the feeling
of common nationhood was very faint, do we find
the relations of the two less cordial, less tinged with
the sense of brotherhood. In feudal times, every
trifling difference meant bloodshed; no land was
ever really at peace; and the horrors of war were
unspeakable. But in our own day the leaders of the
Hungarian patriots proved the strongest champions of
peace in the inter-Parliamentary conference. Classical or mediæval history may, indeed, sometimes
show a greater apparent unity between the inhabitants of distant lands. We have the use of
Latin as a universal medium, for instance, and the
special international relations of feudal chivalry.
But the reason of this was that the history and the
civilisation of those times only touched a limited
aristocracy. And the gulf between the Saxon swine-
herd and the Lombard peasant must have been
enormous. If the uprise of the national idea seems
to have cut up our concept of humanity, it has, in
its turn, immensely increased the depth of that conception in each individual country. And if great distinctions are now recognised between the citizens of
the world, it is because modern thought has conferred
that citizenship on vast numbers of human beings who,
in earlier times, were excluded from it by iron laws.

But even were the ideals of nationality and
humanity in reality opposed, there would yet be
not a little to be said for the former. All great
Art, and all great Literature have ever been national.
The great part of the noble enthusiasms of mankind
and almost all political thought have, likewise, been

informed by the spirit of nationhood. For the aspirations of man seem to require a form for their realization, as the imaginings of the poet require the form of his metre, and that form is the nation. His political wisdom, his love, his self-sacrifice, his longing for beauty cling to that idea and flourish as they cluster about it. It were no trifling thing to abandon such support even though we hoped for a more wide-spread and more uniform crop. And in truth the limited cosmopolitanism of the later Greek and the Roman empires were singularly barren in result.

But in fact nationhood is no more opposed to cosmopolitanism or broad humanity, than family life to nationhood. The narrower circle of ideals and emotions may now and then seem to conflict with the broader, but truly understood their interests are identical. The national idea may best flourish where the family idea flourishes; and so the true welfare of the nation accords best with and promotes the welfare of humanity. It is ever through a false understanding that conflict arises. In primitive times when each family thought that its true interest lay in the murder and robbery of its neighbour, the family idea, no doubt, conflicted with that of the nation. But that is the mental attitude of a remote past. And when nations also shall have come to see that their true interest lies in a peaceful self-development rather than in the murder and robbery of each other, it will be understood that the affection and community of interest that bind together fellow-countrymen, but serve to build up that grand structure in which the varied units of humanity shall dwell in friendship and prosperous peace. It is our hope that Ireland shall be one of those units, developing itself on the lines of nationhood, in all things in the highest degree; that by that development of self it may benefit the whole, and that it may thus show that when truly viewed the loftiest notions of humanity are consistent to the full with the idea of a nation.

OTHER WRITINGS BY ARTHUR CLERY

Leader, 22 June 1907, pp. 279–80.

XXIII.—**Joy of Gold and of Silver.***

TWO green-backs lie upon my table. They are two little volumes of poetry by young Irishmen—*The Golden Joy*, by Thomas M'Donagh, and *Chamber Music* by James Joyce. Mr. M'Donagh's work has been noticed in these columns before. And I am glad to hear that that unsatisfied longing to learn Irish, once a feature of his verse, has now been brought to fruition. Would we could all have done as well. With Mr. Joyce I remember attending an Irish class in the early days of O'Growneyism, but though his sentiments are perhaps not so very different from those of the love-songs of Connacht, I fear there is little trace of Gaelic inspiration in him. And he drinks rather at the fountain of French verse. Mr. M'Donagh, too, strong Gael as he is, is mainly classical in his literary affinities.

The question of the purpose of poetry is raised very strongly by these two books. Wherein shall it seek its love-liness? Beauty and joy is the theme of both writers, and ecstasy their mood; but ecstasy unopaline, not hushful. Of the "Abbey" mood, the Yeatsian strain, the dreamy dusk, Mr. M'Donagh has little, Mr. Joyce none at all. There is no mist in either landscape. The clear vision of joy admits no doubt or hesitation in either. But to Mr. M'Donagh earthly beauty is but a symbol, but a shadow, of the clear seen beauty beyond. The beauty in the mind of God, the joy of the eternal vision towards which the poet's soul still soars, like the soul of Augustine of old:—

> "Now is the season of the Golden Joy,
> Now is the season of the birth of Love—
> The perfect passion of the Heart of God,
> The rapture of the Beauty of the world",
> . . . .

Mr. Joyce's ideas of beauty are, I fear, somewhat different. To him earthly beauty and joy are ends in themselves. Love is the only food for the soul's hunger, sweet passion its true loveliness.

"Alas! some poets have been surely damned!"

sings Mr. M'Donagh; let Mr. Joyce take warning. For the moment I fear he is unrepentant.

[Clery quotes "Goldenhair" in full]

There is no mist about that poem, nor chrysolithe, nor litho-pchrysolithe. But Mr. Joyce can be ecstatic in his simplicity.

[Clery quotes "My dove, my beautiful one" in full]

And here is Mr. M'Donagh's criticism upon such poetry after he has spoken of

> Beauty of Nature and Art
> . . . .
> Beauty of dulcet symphonies low and clear;
> Beauty of beauties that fill the ken
> Till the soul is stifled, faints with delight."

He thus deals with poor Mr. Joyce's be-all and end-all, stern moralist, Mr. M'Donagh:—

> "Beauty of human form and voice,
> Of liquid eyes and blushes and lips,
> Of *golden hair* and brow of white; Human Beauty,
>   that whoso sips
> Doth die to a spirit free . . ."

Now, Mdlle. Goldenhair, you did not expect this. You may go back from your window in a huff, my young lady, this time, as the unmoved transcendentalist passes frowning on his way. Yet might one suspect that one of these days our poet may change his views as to the comparative beauties of symphonies and blushes; *le fainne geal an lae.*

Mr. Joyce has a wonderful mastery over the technique of poetry. It is not without supreme skill that he produces lines of such apparent ease and simplicity, every word in its right place, the whole beautiful in its unadorned charm, with a faint, subtle fragrance of earthly loveliness. Your theorists may write as they will, but men will never tire of tales of love, of descriptions of the loved one's charms whether she wanders by *Loc Leun* or, like Mr. Joyce's heroine at Donneycarney, whether she be *cruitin an mbo* or whether

"She bends upon the yellow keys"
  (of the old piano)
"With shy thoughts and grave, wide eyes and hands,
That wander as they list"—

which privilege did not belong to the *"cailin deas"* aforesaid.

Mr. Joyce flows in a clear, delicious stream that ripples

"In deep cool shadow
At noon of day".

I fear an analyst might find that the stream for all its clear coolness was not uncontaminated, that it swarmed with restless, deadly things, not seen by the naked eye. But shall poets be analysed, shall versed love be put under the microscope? Mr. Joyce complies with none of my critical principles; he is, in truth, entirely earthly, unthinking of the greater and further. Though let me say in justice that the casual reader will find nothing in his verses to object to, nothing incapable of an innocent explanation. But, earthly as he is, he is so simple, so pretty, so alluring, I can't bring myself to chide him. I, for one, shall never order that lady of the locks to cease from her song. I leave the task of chastising the poet of the senses to the stern moralist of their order. And Mr. M'Donagh does so in a really splendid allegory.

> "I dreamt last night . . .
> That travelled far I stood beside a sea,
> Whose pale waves crowding stared head over head
> And mouthed warning inarticulate.
> A whisper from no lips gave me their tale,
> Spirits of Poets they, high called and lost,
> Thus missing half the Man's eternity
> For gaining half the Poet's—joy foregone.
> And there by the drier waste of liquid life
> My feet were set upon a living shore
> Wrought of the souls that never knew the Joy.
> . . . .
> These quiet loved I more than the restless foam.
> And yet the human pity at my heart
> Stirred, and would draw me to that passionate shame.
> But that the joy flamed and the glorious phase
> Burst out beyond me:—the waves wept to hear,
> Wept for the exaltation once their own."

There is an echo of Dante in this. Mr. M'Donagh has "the vision". He is the Fra Angelico or Botticelli, where Mr. Joyce, for all his art, and it is an art lovely, enticing, with an earthly sweetness all its own, is but "Andrea del Sarto", the perfect painter.

Yet, even so, in Mr. Joyce there sounds a deeper chord, a music born of sadness and reflection, that mingles love with death:—

[Clery quotes "Gentle lady, do not sing" in full]

He sees the sad beauty of the grave. He may yet see the beauty of that beyond the grave, and use his remarkable power as an artist in embodying the soul of art.

"The aether of the rapture of High God",

raised on the wings of sorrow to the bright golden light. Yet when you have pointed out to Mr. Joyce that he has not the lofty imagination of Mr. M'Donagh, that he lacks the vision and the soul, when you have poured forth all the condemnation in your philosophy of art, you will steal out and buy a copy, and read it, behind the back of your convictions, for he is simple, human and delightful, all at once.

CHANEL.

* *The Golden Joy* by Thomas McDonagh. O'Donoghue: Gill, 2/6. "Chamber music", by James Joyce. Ellen Mathews, 1/6.

Mayo News, Saturday 14 June 1919, p. 4

XXIV.—**Pearse and Pontius.**

Pearse's work as an educator has an importance far outside the island of Ireland. He faced and fought the whole educational system of the late nineteenth and twentieth centuries. He showed the same courage in this as in all his actions. And to appreciate it you must know what he fought against. I have seen a photograph of his time that shows the young Patrick Pearse as the typical narrow-chested, spectacled Intermediate exhibitioner of the period. As with so many men, his latter life was a reaction against his schooldays.

When I was young I often found it hard to understand the degree of popular disfavour attaching to the career of Pontius Pilate. He seemed to have acted up so closely to all the ideals we were implicitly taught to respect. He had a real sympathy for injustice and oppression, tempered with a reasonable regard for public opinion and a complete respect for authority, above all, a due deliberateness of conduct and perfect control of the emotions. What more could one desire? Yet, somehow, all these great qualities which we were duly taught to admire, failed to obtain the respect of subsequent generations (M. Anatole France excepted). There was something unaccountably wrong somewhere, and Pearse had the insight to perceive that what was wrong with Pontius Pilate was just what was wrong with the education of his time. It had no "light".

It is not easy to express the exact thing at which he aimed. How far he achieved it his schoolboys can tell better than I, who knew him only as a teacher of Irish in the older days, at the Catholic university. I have called it light. You might also name it colour or describe it by terms more closely related to the emotions. It meant this, that there should be something more in education, than being an exhibitioner in this life, and an Indian Civil Servant or a Second Division Clerk in the next. Of course it wasn't the next, but you treated it as if it were. In pre-Pearse days I have heard many a young fellow of seventeen or eighteen laying out his plan of life, on the basis of what would be his pension at sixty-five. I dare say many a one does it still. The needs of a war have already shown most countries that such a mode of thought is intolerable. Pearse saw it long before. He knew that ideals are as necessary as food for sustaining life, whether it be the life of the individual or the nation. And if they are necessary anywhere, they are supremely necessary in training the young. Cautiousness may be the most dangerous form of improvidence, self-restraint the greatest of the vices. And as these things are in themselves, they are far worse when made the basis of a system of teaching. If you strike out the high, the reckless, the colour out of life, you rob it of glory, and three pounds or fifty pounds a week is a poor compensation, even gold lace or ermine into the scale.

Of course the religious ideal had always been taught in Ireland. So much of demiaeval glory remained. And few men strove harder towards it than Pearse himself. But though there has not been an actual divide between religion and education in Ireland—our law not admitting such a process—there has been an effectual legal separation between them. The Intermediate Board and the Commissioners of National Education pay alimony on condition that the two live decently apart. Hence there has never been much danger of religious ideals infecting secular education. The two are shut off into separate compartments.

St. Enda's was the visible means adopted by Pearse to propagate ideals of education, which have a world value. It is generally admitted that he went far to carry them into practice. Plainly no spot on earth is so suited for their continued realisation as that institution which he himself founded, where he himself taught. Whoever seeks to promote Pearse's ideals in education, will naturally turn towards this place, which the master himself chose as their home. He will feel that in anything he does to assist the work of St. Enda's, he is in spirit giving to Patrick Pearse.

ARTHUR E. CLERY.

New Ireland Review, October 1905, pp. 65–74.

XXV.—**The Outlanders of Ulster.**

"The question", says Sir Horace Plunkett, in his book, "which the Nationalists had to answer in 1886 and 1893, and which they have to answer to-day, is this: In the Ireland of their conception, is the Unionist part of Ulster to be coerced or persuaded to come under the new regime?" The question is not an unfair one, and perhaps Sir Horace is right in saying that it has not been very satisfactorily dealt with. In any scheme of Home Rule hitherto considered, the answer would have to be that the eastern part of Ulster was, as the lesser of two evils, to be compelled to submit to an arrangement that it disliked, the hope being none the less entertained that it might soon change its opinion and become as satisfied with Home Rule as the Protestant Church in Ireland has become with Disestablishment. It must be confessed, however, that neither the prospect of coercion nor the hopes of persuasion can be looked upon with entire complacency. And the present article is directed to enquiring whether there might not be some third alternative which would offer a simpler and more satisfactory solution of the difficulty.

The principle in accordance with which all former Home Rule Bills have been drafted is what may be called the Geographical conception of Ireland. According to this view, "Ireland" is the island, and all persons who first see the light within its boundaries are Irishmen, the "Irish-born men" of Davis. As a consequence of this doctrine, a great deal of trouble has been expended in endeavouring to persuade a large number of persons that they should be treated as belonging to a nation, with which it is their fixed purpose to have nothing to do. Hence, likewise, the setting forth of Wellington, Wolseley, and Kitchener, as a parallel in high life for Kelly, Bourke, and Shea, the true sons of that fortunate race which gives warriors to the British army and comic characters to the British stage; whilst all the time those noble heroes, drenched in the perfume of British patriotism, have striven to convince their fellow-countrymen that there no longer clings to them the scent of that Augean stable in which they had the misfortune to be born.

Now, while I strongly question this Geographical conception of Ireland or of the Irish nation, and do not consider either Wellington or Laurence Sterne an Irishman, I do not desire to substitute a purely genealogical or *race* conception in its place. There is no need that a true Irishman should be a Gael, or that his family should extend back to one of the three invasions. The racial test is one that no European nation would stand at the present day, and if it be true, as is now asserted, that the Gaels are sprung from the same ancestors as the Germans, and the English in large part of the same stock as the French, such genealogical classification might lead to very unsuspected results. Consequently, nationality is looked upon throughout the world, not as a matter of pedigree, but as a matter of fact. And there is no reason why a man should not be an Irishman to-day, whether his family be sprung from the Firvolce or the Danes, the Angevins or the Saxons. But while a man named Wesley, or Wellesley, might well be an Irishman, it is equally true that Arthur Wellesley was not; and though thousands of men of English and Scotch descent are to-day Irishmen, we are forced to recognise that there are many more thousands to whom Irish residence and Irish birth have failed to impart that character.

There are, in truth, two means by which a man may become a member of a nation—by birth and by absorption. This latter process, which is the natural equivalent for the artificial and political practice of naturalisation, I recognise quite as freely as the advocates of the geographical idea, but I refuse to admit that the mere fact of birth or residence necessarily implies absorption. I hold that on the facts, as we know them, there is a large and important body of immigrants into our country, who, having never been absorbed, have never become, and possible never will become, portion of the

Irish nation. The geographical notion, which is set over against
this view, is, as is well known, a result of the now antiquated
theories of feudal lawyers. England was, indeed, one of the
last states to abandon the various absurd consequences which
sprang from the artificial doctrine of making a man's national
character depend upon that of the over-lord under whom he
was born. But a truer conception of the idea of a nation has
now happily supplanted these ancient notions, injurious alike
to patriotism and to religious freedom, which at one time
prevailed amongst the states of Europe.

Who, then, are the non-absorbed, the Outlanders in Ireland?
I fear there will be a ready answer on most people's lips; they
will not stop to draw nice distinctions; they will think of the
Irish Times and answer right off "The Protestants". But though
this rough-and-ready distinction is sufficient, I am afraid, for
many practical purposes, it is not a fair one. There are very
many Protestants true Irishmen; would that there were more.
Who would deny the title to Parnell, to Butt, or to the Young
Irelanders? Nay, do not even Castletown, Dunraven, Shawe-
Taylor and the rest, who feel that Ireland is their country and
strive to serve it with such strength of character as they
possess, deserve the title likewise? To my mind a fair minority
of South of Ireland Protestants seem to be Irishmen, and the
rest are, I think, in the long run, convertible and absorbable.
Living scattered among a large Irish population, they have
long been in progress of mental assimilation; but two considerations have hitherto operated on their wills to keep them
apart—their interest in land and their interest in jobbery. The
Land Act must, within a very few years, extinguish the former,
and it will then be the more patriotic of the ex-landlords who
will then remain on in Ireland. As to the latter, the Protestant
interest in jobbery has been greatly impaired by local government, and anything in the nature of Home Rule would, of
course, make it an asset of no value whatsoever. There would
then remain no barrier save that religious hatred which is the
back-wash of devotion, and, after all, the unpaid and isolated
hater is inevitably at a disadvantage.

If we desire to find the true Outlanders, the unabsorbed
and unabsorbable, we must turn northward. When you have
crossed the canal at Newry, you enter their territory. Here it
is no case of isolated half-converts, kept apart through interest,
or even through snobbery, from those with whom they have
much in common. To pass Goraghwood is like crossing the
highest ridge of the Alps. You leave behind you the kindly
people of the South, and come upon the cold and harsh-
tongued members of another nation, for there is scarce more
in common between Austrian and Italian, than between the
denizen of Ireland and of East Ulster. Indeed it is a fact we
must recognise, and we shall be the stronger for doing so, that
we are not the only nation who inhabit Ireland. Just as a
portion of the French nation dwells in Lorraine, as a portion
of the Danish nation dwells in Schleswig-Holstein, as a portion
of the Italian nation dwells in the South Tyrol, so a portion
of the British nation dwells upon our borders in Ulster. They
are not mere isolated units, who must in time surrender to their
surroundings; they are a strong compact mass, inhabiting a
definite portion of territory, with only enough Irishmen
among them to serve as horrible examples— wealthy, bigoted,
and fixed to the soil. Pressure from without can only knit
them closer together; they are capable of living in unity and
common hatred for centuries.

No doubt the patriotic Irishman will think hopefully of
absorption, just as the patriotic Briton hopes to absorb the
Irish. As the Briton thinks of the Scotch, now happily within
the fold, so the Irishman will remember those Danes and
Angevins, foreigners once upon a time, but now become
portion of our national stock. He will hope that if Sigersons
are Irish to-day, so may Saundersons be to-morrow. He will
reflect, too, that but a century ago, when Catholics had no
share in the government of Ireland, when the Gael did not
obtrude himself, the Presbyterian and the Orangeman was far
more ready to think and talk of an Irish nation than he is to-
day. But again we must face facts. Such an absorption may
take place; but there are great difficulties in its way, and the

mere possibility of its not taking place is an immense difficulty in *our* way. The importance of nationality, and the general recognition of its cohesive force, have greatly increased in recent years, as we have seen among ourselves. Were a new colony of Normans or Angevins to be placed in Leinster, even though there were no religious differences, they would be harder to absorb than their predecessors; how much more so the Britons of Ulster. The process of absorption may indeed proceed on either side, but it will be dismally slow, and its consummation far off. If Germany and Austria maintain their present territories, and grant no fresh concessions, it may well happen that in some centuries there will be no French, no Danes, and no Italians within their empires; so, too, there may be but one race in Ireland; but they will have been sad centuries.

At this point another argument of a more passing character, may come to be used. Reference may be made to the recent remarkable declarations; remarkable alike in their seeming adhesion to Irish nationality and to liberal views of the Sloanite Orangemen. I venture to think, however, that too much emphasis has been laid on these resolutions; that they portend, at most, common action on a few points of common interest, and even as regards that section of the Orangemen who approve of them, are no more an indication of a permanent change of attitude than the combination between Catholics and Orangemen in the elections of 1885. If they mean anything more, they cannot really represent the opinion of East Ulster. For it is an insult to the intelligence of the Protestants and Presbyterians of the North, to assume that they would suddenly abandon in a day, and almost without any cause, principles for which they have striven *per fas et nefas*, for twenty years.

Assuming then that East Ulster has the full power of maintaining its national aloofness for a period of indefinite length, and that there is still a reasonable likelihood of its choosing to exercise that power, how are we to meet the difficulty? How should we treat these Outlanders in any scheme of self-government we fashion, or would see fashioned for ourselves? In a word if we would advance to freedom like

Hungary, how shall we deal with our Croatia? Here we must draw very clearly the distinction between East Ulster and the rest; between, if I might so express it, Ulster and Uladh. It is generally agreed that, speaking roughly, a line could be drawn round all the Protestant settlers, the whole non-Irish element, in the North of Ireland, and that if this line were drawn, the number of Catholics inside it, for the most part Catholic residents in Belfast, would not be very large. All within this line is Ulster, a territory inhabited by foreign settlers, and wholly lost to Ireland; without it, and, for the most part, south of a line drawn from Newry to Derry, is Uladh, the ancient national province of Ireland. Whatever happens, Uladh must, of course, remain part of Eire, but is it equally necessary that Ulster, or East Ulster, the home of the alien, should be incorporated? Is there anything to be gained by creating for ourselves, as it were, a new Ireland; an Ireland that shall be a thorn in the side of Eire, as we have been a thorn in the side of Britain? Is there any reason why, when we are asking justice for ourselves, we should seek to compel a body of foreigners, inhabiting a corner of the island, to forego their national heritage, merely that we may improve the outline of our geographical frontier.

> *O si angulus ille*
> *Proximus accedat, qui nunc denormat agellum.*

Have we any greater warrant than the envious Roman?

There will, of course, be a ready answer. To him, who has the geographical conception of nationality, who thinks more of the land than of the people, such a proposition will seem preposterous. Like the French envoy with Bismarck, he will assert that nature has fixed our boundaries and we must not abandon one foot of our sacred soil. The island, Ireland, must, in his view, ever remain a whole. But to the one who thinks rather of the nation than of the land—and this is the view that has been steadily gaining ground of late—it will seem a plain fact that part of our soil is already in alien hands; that nothing but an internecine war, or a still harder task of compulsion and conversion, can restore it to us. And hence it may seem well to recognise our loss, if by so doing we may save the rest and gain our liberty. For Ireland is, as it were, a prisoner in the keeping of Ulster, and though it hurt our dignity and our pockets, might it not be well, in the long run, to obtain our freedom by buying off our gaoler?

As, then, we are now at the parting of the ways, and any further instalment of government, great or small, must be on a national and not a county basis, I propose that in any such arrangement Ireland shall be understood not to include Protestant Ulster, but that the latter shall be separately dealt with. I would have that National line laid down in law which already exists in fact. As, moreover, the line rather bisects counties than runs along their boundaries, some county rearrangement would likewise be necessary, and the town of Newry and, perhaps, the city of Derry, might also have to be divided. The British within the line would be separated from those Irish, with whom they have no link save the common mis-government of Dublin Castle, and would have their affairs administered from London for the future. They would retain existing Irish law, as we did at the Union, but the powers at present vested in the Lord Lieutenant and Chief Secretary would be transferred to the Home Secretary or the appropriate English minister, with, probably, the addition of a special Under Secretary to the Home Department for Ulster. The powers of the various Irish Boards—Education, Agriculture, Local Government, Works—so far as they deal with Ulster, would be administered by the corresponding London departments. Special arrangements would be made for the sitting of permanent Courts of Assize, and, possibly, even a local Court of Appeal in Belfast, which would be a sub-division of the English Judiciary. These broader changes would be accompanied by the necessary modifications in detail. The subsequent history of Ulster, whether the Union with England should continue, whether it would obtain local Home Rule, or whether it would of its own choice again seek union with Ireland, would, of course, depend on the wishes of its inhabitants. The rest of Ireland—a nation no longer divided against itself—would pursue its prosperous course unchecked. Its peaceful inhabitants would now and again read with pity and horror the accounts of riots and disorders among the uncivilised population of western Britain.

Apart from geographical sentiment, two political arguments are likely to be urged against such a proposal, and it will be seen that they bear a striking resemblance to the current English arguments against Home Rule. It will be said on the one hand that Ireland is an economic whole, that its various parts are interdependent, and that we may not sacrifice the richest and the most industrial portion of our country. It will be urged, on the other hand, that we cannot in justice leave our Catholic fellow-countrymen within the line to the mercy of their ancient enemies. As to the first reason, it is, surely, a mistake to consider East Ulster an economic complement to the rest of Ireland. It is far more closely associated with Great Britain, and from an economic point of view, Belfast and the surrounding towns should rather be considered as an integral portion of England and Scotland. Though the largest industries in the island are in Belfast, yet the interests of a country trying to develop industries are by no means identical with those of a town which merely desires a policy of *laissez-faire* for those industries of long standing it already possesses. Indeed, it may be truthfully stated that Belfast takes, and is likely to take, no share in the industrial revival of Ireland, and is, in fact, almost as much apart from the industry as from the agriculture of the rest of Ireland. Again, even as to the riches of the North, income-tax and other statistics show that its comparative superiority to Leinster and Munster in that respect has been greatly exaggerated.

There remains the question of the East Ulster, and principally the Belfast, Catholics. To them, no doubt, a very real hardship would accrue, as they have ever been strenuous in Nationalist politics. But in the circumstances the question may well be merely whether they are to suffer the hardship of un-Irish government alone or in common with the whole of their fellow-countrymen. They will, at any rate, be no worse off than the much larger body of Irishmen, some of them Gaelic-speaking Irishmen, who have migrated to Glasgow as they have to Belfast. Finally, it may be remarked that to many Belfast Catholics separation from Ireland will be the less heavy, as a process of absorption has been going on, and their nationality has been almost fined down to politics alone. Whence it has come to pass that no body of Catholic Irishmen have, as a whole—with some remarkable exceptions—shown themselves less receptive of Gaelic League ideas than those who inhabit Belfast. Whether any reciprocal arrangements for the Catholics of Belfast and the Protestants of Dublin, any setting-off of the Falls Road against Rathmines, could be entered into is a question of too great detail to be considered here, but seems capable of affording matter to the humorist.

It may be interesting to recall that a proposal of separate treatment of Ulster was one of the conditions on which Mr. Joseph Chamberlain offered, whether honestly or dishonestly, to agree to autonomy for Ireland in 1886; Matthew Arnold also favoured such a solution. The coming abolition of the landlord interest, needless to say, immensely simplifies the difficulties which had then to be met with. But when separate treatment is proposed in Ulster it should, of course, be East Ulster and not Uladh. I mention these facts to show that if my proposals are not entirely novel, neither can they be deemed entirely fantastic. The principle that underlies them is merely that of doing unto others as we would have done unto ourselves, of recognizing the national principles and prejudices of our East Ulster enemies as we would have our own nationality recognized by England. No doubt, the difficulties in detail are considerable, and any such solution will have against it the dislike of practical men for complicated schemes and the hatred with which we all view any proposed modification in an ingrained idea. Unionists may think there is too much nation, and nationalists too much union in the proposal, and yet, again, they may both think there is too little. But it is never worth while crushing men's spirits for the sake of administrative simplicity. That is the policy of Russia. If we can prove that Irish freedom causes bondage to no man we shall have done much to help forward our cause. The arguments against Home Rule have hitherto been three—the landlord argument, the Ulster argument, and the Empire argument. The first is fast disappearing. If we can remove the second we shall easily be able to show that the third really makes in our favour. Looking at the matter from our own side, we shall have stooped to conquer; we shall have given up an imaginary part to save the real whole; we shall have abandoned the ideal of Davis and put aside the hopes of many generations of Nationalists. To a sentimentalist this is a great deal. But, on the other hand, we shall have made the boundary of our country coincide with that of our people; we shall have preserved and strengthened our national forces by concentrating them; we shall have shown the true unity of Ireland by separating from those who have no right to that title; we shall have lost some linen mills and ship-building yards, some rope-walks and tobacco factories; we shall have abandoned a good many square miles of indifferent land; but we shall, as against that, have strengthened both our forces and our cause, and shall, at the price of their full freedom, have purged from out our nation a disaffected body of turbulent and bigoted aliens.

ARTHUR SYNAN.

Leader, 9 February 1918, pp. 11–12.

XXVI.—**Armagh Virumque.**

I am getting a little tired of the Ulster Catholic. He takes the wrong side with such inevitable iteration. He has rounded on Sinn Fein. He rounded on Parnell. The glories of Justin McCarthy appealed to him. "Tenant Right" was before my time. I don't know its rights and wrongs. But in my time there never was a bit of mean crawling to the other side to be done, that your East Ulster Catholic did not seem ready to do it. Much of what he does may be protected from criticism by D.O.R.A. But this much isn't, that his great object is to be as like the Protestants as it is possible to be without losing his immortal soul. He plays "Soccer" instead of Irish games, because the Protestants play "Soccer". They repay this imitation by taking pot shots at him with revolvers. He sings music hall airs, because the Protestants sing music hall airs. He has a white horse in his possession because they have a white horse in theirs. His dances must be unpatriotic dances, because theirs are unpatriotic. He despises Irish, because the settlers who live around him despise it. He expects his M.P. to be a centre of jobbery, because the Unionist M.P. is. That is why you get the impression of being in a foreign country whenever you go north of Newry. Their virtues are their own; they have two; they are pious and they fight well in a riot. Their vices are their enemies', copied as nearly as possible.

Of course there are a fair number of men among East Ulster Catholics, who have broken with the tradition, men who have the moral courage to be Irish, who don't cringe and sneak to the other side and hurry off to give them their professional business at the first opportunity. (The other side reply by kicking them.) But these men of bolder ideas and new courage are not the normal men. They are an unpopular though doubtless increasing minority.

The matter is one for the Ulster man himself, but there is a point where we come in. We are dragged at the tail of these East Ulster Catholics who perpetually sneak on us and betray us, who even ally themselves with the Orangemen against us. We must, we are told, submit to have a new Protestant ascendancy set up over us by Lord Midleton and his friends in the South and West, we must give up all real hope of freedom, fiscal or political, so that we may not lose the Ulster Catholic, so that we may save him from his Ulster allies. This I suppose is the current doctrine of Sinn Fein, though the ablest intellect of the Sinn Fein Party, the Swift of Crossna, took a different view. Well, Sinn Fein has had its first taste of Ulster, both Ulsters, Catholic and Protestant; there is a marvellous unity between them. East Ulster has struck its blow in our faces. South Armagh was a district I would have saved from the Orange clutch, or fought to save. It has declared its self-determination to Ireland and Irish America. People often say to me that they cannot understand how one who sympathises as much as I do with the Sinn Fein point of view, could ever have envisaged partition. My answer is South Armagh. I am sick of being tied to Carson by Catholics, tied to England by Carson. The Ulster Catholics have taken Carson to their bosom, let him take them to his bosom. Even Davis never included Irish-born men, who were not to Ireland true. And Davis came from the South. I know these are not the ideas of Sinn Fein. They are my ideas.

CHANEL.

Leader, 8 August 1931, pp. 32–6.

XXVII.—**Corkery's Synge.**

Belloc wrote on the path to Rome. I am writing this on the
way to Lough Derg—shall I get there?—in fact these actual
words are being penned in Dundalk Station. I have just now
been admiring the Mourne Mountains, seen across the water.
But my purpose is not to write of the things I see around me,
but rather of Professor Corkery's book, his new book about
J. M. Synge. At first sight, it seems a strange combination,
one of the most native writers, writing about him who has
been taken as their leader by the "Ascendancy". The word
is Professor Corkery's, and he is careful to distinguish "ascendancy" writing, on the one hand, from "native" writing in
English, from Gaelic literature and from the brilliant productions of the expatriated Irish cosmopolitans, such as Bernard
Shaw and George Moore.

The truth is probably that though we rail at the whole
tribe of ascendancy and cosmopolitan writers, we generally
have a favourite or two among them. Personally I favour the
poems, and not the politics, of Yeats, and the plays of Lennox
Robinson (I place him much below T. C. Murray, however).
I am willing to make a present of all that Synge, AE, and
Sean O'Casey ever wrote. I mildly admire one or two things
by Lady Gregory. The rest of them are to me not worth
mentioning.

Professor Corkery, while having no particular liking for
Yeats or Lennox Robinson, or O'Casey, or, I fancy, even for
T. C. Murray, gives his every vote for Synge. It is probably
not much more reasoned a preference than my own liking for
Thackeray and O. Henry; but reasons in full are given here.
Corkery admits that Synge was one of the "ascendancy" in
the fullest sense, but will have it that he was saved from
ascendancyism by his studies of the people, made while living
among them. He admits, however, that Synge turned an

absolutely blind eye to the religious sentiments of the people, and to this extent all his work is out of focus, that he succeeded in making men and women who, like the characters of Dickens, never existed, is admitted. All Synge's people are without conscience, and therefore practically without real characters. They are said by people who know the Arran Islanders to have only a faint relation to the islanders, from whom they are for the most part drawn. They speak a marvellously vivid dialogue, a species of prose poetry, couched in a dialogue that never was on earth. The attraction of wholly non-moral people speaking this strange tongue caught the taste of Europe and made Synge famous in his time. O'Casey did much the same thing with the speech of the Dublin tenements in our own day. Opinion has now hardened on the fact that Synge's dialect is as false to life as the picture he draws. Men neither speak like Synge, or act like Synge's characters in any part of Ireland. He was in fact something like Turner, the painter, a brilliant unrealist. And we can scarcely complain of the originals being hurt by the caricature.

I remember an account of the first night of "the Playboy" I got from the late R.J. Kinahan, the barrister, just after it. Kinahan was brilliant, but rather a conventional man, quite ready to enjoy "a good story" like most men of his type. He said that the play gave the audience the impression of being not anti-Irish, but anti-human; and, of course, we all know how the audience rose at the phrase about ladies in their night attire as detailed by Corkery. I saw the play much later, and was surprised there had been so much pother about it. "Riders to the Sea", a much better play, I saw either the first night or soon afterwards. I remember it gave me the effect of a visit I had once paid to a dissecting room, but the man with me was greatly impressed. Corkery says that it is distinguished from Synge's other work by a glint of Christianity breaking through it, but the main theme is that the hopeless fight against the sea is as pagan a motif as anything in Synge's work and perhaps less obviously offensive. As a tragedy, however, it is certainly effective.

Professor Corkery is of course right in stressing the fact that Synge died young. Had he lived to share the political enthusiasms of the next ten years, getting some idea of moral values the while, he might have won more enduring fame. His is all the time the work of a young man, influenced by the anti-moral tone of his artistic surroundings; perhaps he was to some extent in revolt against the ultra-moral and almost Jansenist tone of his favourite author, Racine. For he was one of the very few English-speaking men who had a real appreciation for that writer.

Even those who may not be greatly interested in Synge will find much to attract them in Professor Corkery's volume. He writes frankly from a "native" point of view throughout, and is prepared to incur the penalty of loss of publicity and practical suppression which such a view entails. I need not tell readers of this journal how such suppression is brought about. Thirty years' boycott and silence has been the result of our labours, and any man who is unwilling to sneak to ascendancy and anti-Christianity will meet the same fate, to be ignored and forgotten by his fellow-Christians. For the anti-Christian forces are, if anything, stronger in such matters and have more influence among Christians than even in matters of jobbery. He who writes Christian and writes well will write for the Irish alone, and for a very small class among them. Such a man is Daniel Corkery. My congratulations, therefore, to the Cork College for having chosen such a man as its teacher of literature.

CHANEL.

[There is a commercial term which, if our memory serves us rightly, is "Errors and omissions excepted". We would like to add that term to our contributor's article, as he, being on the way to St. Patrick's Purgatory, there is no chance of his revising his proof. The only handwriting we can compare in the matter of illegibility to that of "Chanel" was that of the late Dr. McWalter. We usually spend from half to a whole hour dressing up "Chanel's" script for the compositor, and then we leave over a few conundrums for the compositor. Between us, when we get back his proof we may safely say that both experts in illegible handwriting, ourselves and the compositor, have not correctly interpreted his scrawl, and there are corrections to be made. In a covering letter our contributor says: "Dear D. P., as I am on the way to Lough Derg and Bundoran, a proof will be impossible. You must do as best you can", so the article is published, "errors and omissions excepted"—Ed. L.]

Leader, 2 June 1917, pp. 400–1.

XXVIII.— **Dog-Collars and Conventions.**

It is often forgotten in our time that Tone, Emmet and Fitzgerald died in the cause of Democracy. Nationality was only their second motive. Democracy was then a new and great thing in the world, as it is to-day in Russia. And men like Tone and Emmet were proud to be its martyrs. They had about as much in common with Grattan and the Whigs of the Protestant Ascendancy as James Connolly had with John Redmond. It is the irony of fate that their names should now-adays often be associated with those of their bitterest opponents. If Tone or Emmet were alive to-day they would rise against any Whig Government set up in our midst, just as they did in their own time. There is this much only of difference, that democracy, which was a new thing in their day, has now won out in the world.

   The reason for re-stating these obvious truths is that there is now a powerful and well-supported conspiracy afoot to establish an anti-democratic system of government in Ireland. When the rest of the world is turning towards Democracy, it is hoped to make Ireland march in the opposite direction. At one time only O'Brienites and a handful of Conservative dissidents held these views. Now the propaganda is more widespread. It is hoped to make the proposed Conference an instrument for carrying them out. The wolf-hound will be let out on a chain. He is to wear a Protestant dog-collar. He will be released from confinement on these terms. Tone and Emmet did not die for dog-collars. Freedom and democracy were the objects alike of those patriots whose names are allowed and of those whose names are not allowed to be mentioned.

   Ireland won't have it, and what is more Ulster won't have it. They have almost as little sympathy with the Southern Ascendancy gang as we have. They don't mind their governing us, but they have no love for them. You cannot conciliate

Ulster by giving fancy franchises to landlords or Castle hacks. People have often wondered that I hold the views about Ulster I do. One strong reason is that I loathe and abominate the proposed alternative to partition, a Whig-cum-Protestant Government imposed on Ireland. Almost the only achievement of constitutional agitation in Ireland, of Davitt, Biggar, and Parnell, was that it cleared out these people, with all their corruption once and for all, or rather it hemmed them in between Kingstown and Dublin Castle (Holyhead is the next move). Are we now going to bring them back? While political liberty has so far made no advance in Ireland, democracy and economic liberty have made great strides. The whole Irish population is still as it were in a dungeon, but Irish natives no longer wear special chains. It is frequently proposed nowadays that we should put on these chains again of our own accord (much as O'Connell did to pass Emancipation) as the price of union with Ulster. I do not believe Ulster desires such a bargain; it is the Whig and the "South and West" who demand it. But even if Ireland could come to such terms, Ascendancy is too great a price to pay for Independence. As it is we have one piece of good fortune; the bigotry of the North will probably save us from being enslaved to the crueller but more plausible bigotry of the South.

Let me say it frankly, the partitionist principle is inevitable in any real solution of the Irish problem upon lines of representative government. This is equally true whether the solution be the handiwork of Ireland or of the British Government or of foreign Powers. You can postpone its application as long as you like—public opinion demands this course—even for another century—but you can come to no real settlement without it. You cannot make one democracy out of Ireland and Ulster; you can at best govern them by a single ascendancy. But much can be done to reconcile the partitionist principle with national unity, if Ireland will concede something of unity, Ulster something of liberty, England something of sovereignty. None of them need concede any point of democracy. Lloyd George's unpopular alternative scheme is only a first faint-hearted

attempt in this direction. A solution within the British Empire
might be found on lines such as the following:

> The King of England, crowned with the crown of his
> ancestors, the O'Neills at Tara, and having a palace there,
> would function as a constitutional High King for Ireland,
> acting on the advice of an All-Ireland (or Commonwealth)
> ministry, chosen by an All-Ireland (or Commonwealth)
> Parliament, itself elected on a democratic franchise. Under
> this Commonwealth Government and owing allegiance to
> it would be two provincial governments and legislatures,
> constituted on a democratic basis, the Irish Republic with
> its President, and the Principality of Ulster, with its Prince
> or Viceroy. The exact confines of the governments of
> O'Connell Street and Donegall Place could be peacefully
> determined by a plebiscite and the Local Government
> Board. The flag of the Tara Government—Tara is the
> Irish Delhi—would be orange and green with an Irish
> crown. To this the Dublin government would add white.
> The Belfast Government would leave out the green and
> add a red hand. The Ulster and Irish Governments would
> each have their own volunteers, but the supreme command
> of both would be under the Tara Government. The Tara
> assembly need not necessarily meet at Tara after the first
> time, it might for instance move about like the Oireachtas.
> Appeals from the courts of Dublin and Belfast would go,
> not as it is at present enacted, to the English Privy Council,
> but to the Supreme Court at Tara, a body to be chosen
> under some circumstances of impartiality. This is the merest
> outline, variable in every point, but it is the sketch of an
> eminently practical possibility, meeting racial and national
> sentiment and wholly consonant with democratic principles.

CHANEL.